Since his days at LaGrange Colle̶ pas has been an 'unstoppable' fo̶r̶c̶e̶.̶ ̶E̶v̶e̶n̶ ̶t̶h̶e̶n̶,̶ ̶h̶e̶ ̶s̶h̶o̶w̶e̶d̶ ̶g̶r̶e̶a̶t̶ promise as a successful musician, theologian, minister, and husband. He lives by the principles he explains to be successful. Prepare to be inspired by Antipas' life and his writing that you, too, might become an 'unstoppable' force for good in the world.

> —F. STUART GULLEY, PH.D., Past President of LaGrange
> College, President of Woodward Academy in Atlanta, GA

Dr. Antipas Harris, a young, black, and gifted theologian from the clay hills of rural Georgia, called of God to serve the refused of this present age, is a breath of fresh air with a desire to see the hard-core inner-city demographic changed through the power of values-driven success. Harris boldly goes where others stay safely away. He takes the reader from his previous seminal work on the Holy Spirit in *Holy Spirit, Holy Living* to this current volume on *Unstoppable Success*. Harris stands boldly and offers a word in due season: 'If I am saved, can I experience abundant life that includes both life in the great beyond as well as success here in the urban jungle or suburban whitewash?' Harris' answer is resounding through the pages of this book, 'Yes, you can.' You can experience irresistible success in the face of insurmountable adversity. This work is a cry, anthem, and praise echoed across the Kingdom of Jesus Christ for this generation and generations to come. Read every jot and tittle of this book!

> —REV. FRANCYS JOHNSON, J.D., Attorney and Counselor at
> Law, President of Georgia State Conference of the NAACP

Antipas Harris empowers us to reconcile the optics of faith with the metrics of success in a manner that goes beyond impacting. It changes lives!

> —REV. SAMUEL RODRIGUEZ, President of NHCLC, Hispanic
> Evangelical Association

I predict that this book is going to be unstoppably successful. A more encouraging and empowering read hasn't come around in a long while.

—REV. JAMES "JIM" WOOD, Senior Pastor of First Presbyterian Church (Norfolk, VA)

You can have skills. But, when you have character, you have greatness. Antipas teases out both the meaning of success and principles that will help you get there. Showing all of us that, in spite of life's challenges, we can be unstoppable. Let's keep pressing towards the higher mark! Antipas speaks from his heart to our hearts. Antipas is a people-person with both a powerful and a palpable message for the people. It has been said, 'I'd rather see a sermon any day than hear one.' Antipas paints the image of success in a way that we can see it.

—MICHAEL "MOSES" MATHIS, Multiple Grammy, Dove, & Stellar Award-Winning, Producer & Musician, President of Jamdo Jamdo Music

The journey of life is not easily traversed, and few have done so successfully. Dr. Antipas Harris has been blessed with phenomenal success in many aspects of his life, and now he has graciously shared his success principles with others. I encourage you not only to read this book but also to apply the principles contained herein. You will not be disappointed.

—REV. ALFRED D. WATTS, Senior Pastor, Cornerstone Christian Center in Milford, CT

UNSTOPPABLE SUCCESS

*7 Ways to Flourish in
Your Boundless Potential*

DR. ANTIPAS L. HARRIS

G/I\E\L\D
academic
press

GIELD Academic Press

To the Disciples at
The Union Mission Ministries Men's
Shelter In Norfolk, VA;
To the Guests at The Center: A Temporary
Shelter in Norfolk, VA.

CONTENTS

ABOUT THE AUTHOR

From humble beginnings in the clay hills of Manchester, GA, Antipas Harris has traveled throughout parts of Europe, South America, North America, and Africa, speaking, teaching, and preaching in schools, leadership centers, arenas, and churches. Harris currently serves on the full-time faculty at Regent University in Virginia Beach, VA.

In Spring of 2013, Harris was awarded the Regent University Award for Excellence in Service. In Fall of 2012, he was named by the *International Top 100 Magazine* as a top 100 International Leader for his work in urban ministry, higher education, and community outreach. In 2011, he was named to the Wall of Outstanding Alumni at his alma mater, LaGrange College. Harris was also named to the 2011 *Inside Business* "Top 40 Under 40" of Hampton Roads.

Harris holds a DMin from Boston University, STM from Yale University, MDiv from Emory University, and a BA from LaGrange College where he graduated with cum laude honors.

Antipas is happily married to Micah. Micah shares his love for teaching and the arts. She is a skilled modern dancer and currently serves as an elementary school assistant principal in Virginia Beach, VA. Together, Antipas and Micah live in Virginia Beach, VA.

GRATITUDE

I HAVE ENJOYED SHARING the concepts presented in this book at high schools, colleges, universities, churches, in seminars, in classes, and with the discipleship group at the Union Mission Men's Shelter in Norfolk, VA. I owe a debt of gratitude to each of the students, disciples, and congregants who have challenged me to think deeply and to reflect intensely on the concepts in this book.

I wish to thank several people who have helped me along the way to learn and grow as a person, a preacher, and a scholar. To only mention a few, I want to thank my dear wife, Micah, for your love and support. I love you more than words can express. I would like to thank my parents, Pastor James and Carolyn Harris, and my siblings for your support over the years. This book is also a tribute to all of my mentors and teachers.

Thanks to Darren Shearer of High Bridge Books and my proofreaders, Sebrina Brown and Min. Jerry Adatsi, along with Micah, for helping me to bring this manuscript to its current form. A special thanks to Zachery A. Smith, Sr. for making the best out of the image you saw through the lens of your camera. May the Lord bless your business!

Additionally, I wish to thank my colleagues at Regent University and so many others for your inspiration over the years, including kind "friends" from around the world who follow me through social media.

Importantly, I would like to thank you, the reader, for taking the time to read and ponder what I have to say in the pages ahead. I hope that you find hope and help in the message of these truths.

Most importantly, I want to thank God. If it had not been for the Lord, where would we be? Glory to the Lord Jesus! He has done great things. True success comes from the Lord of the universe. This means that success is a universal possibility. It does not belong to a selected few, privileged people in certain clusters of the planet, but to everyone, regardless of race, ethnicity, gender, social location, or geographical environment.

INTRODUCTION

SUCCESS IS ON MANY PEOPLE'S MINDS these days. The meaning of *success* may vary a little from person to person, but for the most part, we tend to associate the word *success* with finances or some sort of material gain.

Recently, I was sitting at the gate in the Tampa, Florida airport, waiting to board a flight to Norfolk. I looked to my right and noticed a book in a lady's hand. I looked closer to see the name of the book. It was Darren Hardy's, *The Compound Effect: Jumpstart Your Income, Your Life, Your Success.* While I did not ask her why she was reading the book, I am not surprised that anyone would be reading that type of book to learn more about how to succeed financially. Times are challenging on the financial front. Darren Hardy built a company, which earned him nearly $50 million by the age of twenty-seven. He definitely has something to say about making money that is probably worth listening to.

Yet, while we alert our attention to brilliant entrepreneurs like Hardy, Bill Gates, Mark Zuckerberg, and others, let's not forget that money is fleeting. When foundations are enduring, material achievements are complementary to true success. However, material gain does not define the fundamental essence of success.

The heart of true success consists of hope, joy, peace, and love. The question becomes, "How do we get to the heart of the matter?" I believe that true success results from an underpinning of godly standards, practical principles that every one of us should apply in our lives every day. When we build our lives on the Lord, we position ourselves for true success.

True success is, also, holistic. My youngest brother and emerging music producer, D. Arcelious Harris (R' Celious the Producer), recently posted a Facebook status, "I've learned to stop chasing my ambitions to become whatever and whomever God has blessed me to see myself as."[1] Importantly, chasing ambitions without insight into what God has for us leads to an exercise of futility. However, there is great fulfillment in seeking first the kingdom of God and His righteousness. Material success can only then be properly added (*ref.* Matthew 6:33).

I am sure that you have deep-rooted passions that give way to your particular ambitions. But, perhaps, you have felt rejected along the way. Or, maybe you have found success hard to reach because of some learning curve, knowledge deficiency, or character flaw. I have been there.

Or, possibly, you have struggled due to pain, abuse, traumatic experiences, or addictions. You feel that you have made too many poor choices to become anything worthwhile.

Or, you may feel that you are too old now. Or, maybe you feel that you are a good age, but your situational, social, or geographical locale makes success impossible for you. You have always dreamed of success, but life has dealt you such a hard blow that the reality of success seems impossible. You have either given up, or you have decided just to settle in the wilderness of mediocrity. If you identify with any of these categories, this book is for you. If you know anyone who may be in either of these situations, this book is for them.

I want to lay a foundation for revitalized dreams of success, encourage you in the journey, and even in some cases catapult you toward a Christ-centered pursuit of goals and objectives.

Let me begin by explaining what success is not. Success does not equal stuff. The essence of a diamond can't be reduced to the "bling" of shiny stuff. It is the quality of the building blocks with which the diamond is constructed. No diamond is successfully a diamond without the pressure that compounds it under the dirt.

Relating the diamond to success, the essence of success is the building blocks that create it. In keeping with the journey metaphor, in the pages ahead, the steps of the journey are the real meaning of success. Those building blocks, those steps that are so meaningful for success, are rooted and grounded in God's Word. They are constructive principles upon which we can build our lives. They are renewing principles that will turn our lives around if we are headed in the wrong direction. They serve as a springboard to catapult us toward a success that the world can't give, and the world can't take away. It is a God-ordained and God-given success.

Principles are formational, enduring values that form our way of being and doing in the world. When we don't have firm principles that form us, we simply exist. Indeed, there are many people who are good at what they do in terms of professional activity. The deeper concern is more than one of profession but one of formation. In other words, success requires that we don't just develop skills in a profession but that we become fully formed in Christ. The fullness of success rests in formational principles along with—or, at times, even more so—skill development. For example, these days, many employers would hire an honest person with minimal skills but with potential for development rather than a skillful person with proof of little integrity. Countries as well as employers are looking for ethical integrity because they have come to realize that skills alone don't produce long-term success.

In the famous book, *The Seven Habits of Highly Effective People,* Stephen R. Covey comments on how the life-support factors of success (wisdom, security, guidance, and power) depend upon a foundation of strong principles. He explains,

> By centering our lives on correct principles, we create a solid foundation for development… Principles are deep, fundamental truths, classic truths, and generic common denominators. They are tightly interwoven threads running with exactness, consistency, beauty, and strength through the fabric of life… Even in the midst of people or circumstances that seem to ignore the principles, we can be secure in the knowledge that principles are bigger than people or circumstances, and that thousands of years of history have seen them triumph, time and time again. Even more important, we can be secure in the knowledge that we can validate them in our lives, by our own experience.[2]

As a Christian, I believe that "correct" principles are "Christ-centered" values. True success is the integration of Christ-centered principles with passionate energy toward personal and communal fulfillment.

I offer this book as a step toward a practical theology of success—"practical" because success is not an esoteric idea. Success is experienced and enjoyed. I wish above all that you prosper in every way and that you get the most out of life.

Also, this book is very much "theological" because true success is fundamentally a God-related matter. I want to encourage you in your walk with the Lord. To have "stuff" or to reach a goal in life is only part of what success is about. We need a spiritual relationship with God to discover our greatest potential, to reach that potential, and to have peace and joy from beginning to end.

For several years, I have pondered the questions, "What is true success, and how do I achieve it?" I have wrestled with this question in sermons and lectures in different parts of the world. In those moments of sharing, I have not claimed full grasp of the subject. While I continue to discover the depth of a God-kind of success, I have tried to share some foundational insights at churches, schools, and other venues that I also extend to you in the pages ahead.

In 2010, I visited Port-au-Prince, Haiti at the invitation of Pastor Pierre Louis, a former student at Regent University's School of Divinity. While in Haiti, I had the opportunity to share at Bellevue Salem Baptist Church II's Annual Youth Conference. So, I shared on some of the keys to success. For a full week, I was privileged to offer a different key each night. I spoke for 45 minutes or so and then sat in front of the church to entertain questions from the audience. I was particularly intrigued by how seriously the young people engaged the subject. The best way that I can describe it is that they impressed me with their hunger for knowledge. They listened intensely and took copious notes.

During the question and answer session, they did not hesitate to approach the microphone with their questions. Each of them asked questions that would help them to achieve their greatest potential for their lives. After sharing in Port-au-Prince, Haiti, the senior pastor (who is also an attorney), Rev. David VILMA, asked me to consider penning these keys to success for others to glean inspiration and direction in their pursuit of success.

Miles to Go

Twentieth-Century American writer, Robert Frost, used "journey" as a metaphor about life. Two of his poems have stuck in my head since high school: "The Road Not Taken" and "Stopping by Woods on a Snowy Evening." In many ways and at different times in my life, these poems have inspired my life's journey. As pertaining to my quest for success, the last stanza of "Stopping by Woods on a Snowy Evening" reminds me that the road to success is not quick. It is long and sometimes arduous:

> The woods are lovely, dark, and deep,
> But I have promises to keep,
> And miles to go before I sleep,
> And miles to go before I sleep.

While there are many attractions in life, lots of mysteries to explore, and countless ideas to unearth, at this stage of my life, I am interested in the specific avenues through which God will guide me to achieve His will. I have miles to go before I achieve the kind of success that God has in store.

To borrow Paul's words in Philippians 3:13-14, "I don't consider that I have made it myself. But... straining forward to what lies ahead, I press on toward the goal for the prize of the upward call of God in Christ Jesus." Paul is speaking about eternal success more so than mere earthly accomplishments. By "eternal," he is explaining the qualities that are essential to life both now and the life that is to come. He isn't speaking only about temporal matters for earthly advantages, alone. I believe, moreover, that Paul's principles of pursuing the higher calling are fitting for both finite and infinite accomplishments.

In this book, I will explain Christ-centered success that is conditioned by selfless commitment to godly principles of faith, vision, education, humility, persistence, connections, and honesty. I draw mainly from selected Scriptures, teachings from childhood, testimonies, valuable lessons in my journey, and African American folklore. While this book is not an exhaustive treatment on the subject, I believe that these few nuggets from meaningful sources of support and from my own journey will inspire you.

Philosophically Speaking

In 1994, philosopher and religious scholar, Tom Morris, offered a philosophical view of "true" success. Morris' book, *True Success*, was born out of his approach and positive results in helping athletes at the University of Notre Dame to excel in his Philosophy course.[3] In *True Success*, Morris offers seven foundational conditions for success. He calls them the "7 Cs": a *conception* of what we want, a *confidence* to see us through, a *concentration* on what it takes, a *consistency* in what we do, a *commitment* of emotion, a *character* of high quality, and a *capacity* to enjoy. Similar to my writing approach here, each of Morris' chapters explains one of these conditions. Morris believes that these conditions (or what I call, "principles") could be the missing ingredients of true success in many of life's contexts, including business, ministry, education, and more. He calls the book "a new philosophy of excellence."[4]

Morris' new philosophy of excellence is about the condition of one's attitude. We achieve excellence based on our attitude both *before* we set foot to the journey as well as *while* we are on the pathway to achieving it. I find it apropos that Morris would point out the importance of conditioning one's self for excellence.

In Scripture, Paul also advises the believers in Philippi, suggesting the need for positive thinking. Historically, the Christian Church was experiencing strong opposition and severe treatment. Paul, himself, was writing to them from jail. He was incarcerated for preaching the gospel. How awful! Yet, Paul's most optimistic letter in the New Testament is this very letter to the Philippians during persecution. How could this be possible? Paul responds to this rhetorical question saying,

> Finally, brothers [and sisters], whatever is true, whatever is honorable, whatever is just, whatever is pure, whatever is lovely, whatever is commendable, if there is any excellence, if there is anything worthy of praise, think about these things. (Phil. 4:8)

Philosophically speaking, excellence has to do with how we think about both the challenges as well as the goal to which we aspire.

Morris points out that the main positive attitude related to all successful people is the realization that "true success is up to them."[5] I hasten to mention that this condition or attitude of taking responsibility in no way replaces reliance on God. It is, rather, a human awareness that God has given us free will to choose success or to reject it. If we choose success, we must pursue it in a godly way, yet we need proactivity if we are to be successful.

The next condition that I want to emphasize is faithfulness. Mother Teresa pointed out to biographer Navin Chawla, "We are called upon not to be successful, but to be faithful."[6] This is deep! One way to read Mother Theresa's comment on faithfulness is as a wise lesson on true friendship with God, what Bishop B. Courtney McBath calls, "living at the next level." Bishop McBath says,

> Our friendship with [Jesus] is our Next Level – the place where we find true fulfillment. We can get off track in life waiting for some spectacular breakthrough, some big miracle moment when we finally "arrive" and all of our dreams come true... Becoming God's friend is our breakthrough.[7]

Faithfulness in our relationship with the Lord situates success deep within our souls. In the pages ahead, I will explain some key Christ-centered principles that help us to orient our souls such that, no matter the roadblocks and mishaps in life, our souls are satisfied.

I have noticed at least three categories to which people belong on this issue of success and the orient of the soul. First, some people have very little in terms of material possessions. But, like Saint Francis of Assisi, Mother Teresa, and countless others who have forsaken earthly treasures and have chosen a vow to poverty, their souls are satisfied with Jesus. In a deeply meaningful way, people in this category are profoundly successful.

Second, some people possess a lot of material wealth: fame, houses, cars, money, assets, etc. But, like one of the first Mexican actresses Lupe Velez; rock star, Kurt Donald Cobain; famous "Soul Train" Television Show mogul, Don Cornelius; the multi-millionaire and husband of "Housewives Beverly Hills" star, Russell Armstrong; and others who became deeply troubled for one reason or the other and committed suicide, they have worldly possessions and notoriety, but their souls are just not satisfied.

Third, there are those who maintain a deep spirituality. They are in love with Jesus. But, at the same time, they are climbing up the ladder of material achievement. They take seriously Ecclesiastes 10:19c, which states, "money answers everything." Yet, they are not in love with money. They put their love for Christ first in their order of priorities. Similarly to Abraham in the Bible, they work hard, produce wealth, and they are friends with God. Their success is then twofold, both material and spiritual (or *quantifiable* and *soulish*). Yet, the richness of both their *quantifiable* and *soulish* productivity is rooted deeply in their faithful relationship with God. I wish to locate the teachings in this book closest to this third category.

Stated differently, the call to faithfulness implies a divine concern for something similar to what Aristotle calls *eudaimonia*, a human happiness that centers on holistic thriving. In *Nicomachean Ethics*, Aristotle explains happiness or *eudaimonia* as "living well and doing well."[8] I understand Aristotle's ethic of happiness in terms of a non-hedonistic attitude of holistic flourishing or thriving. It is from this basic philosophical trajectory that I begin the following discussion of success.

Theologically Speaking

Each of us has a calling from God. As pertaining to "divine calling," pastor and author Ruth Haley Barton draws from Moses' experience at the burning bush and comments,

> When God calls, it is a very big deal. It is holy ground. It produces within us such reverence and awe that it is hard to know what to do with ourselves. Finally the whole of our life begins to make sense, and new awareness of that divine orchestration that has brought us to this moment makes us want to take off our shoes or fall on our face or maybe even argue with God about the improbability of it all... Every single thing that didn't make sense when it happened, that seemed too harsh or too random or too shameful, now finds its place in the storyline that brought us here.[9]

As majestic, exciting, and important as it may be, a calling is only the beginning. Where do we go from here? What are we called to do? True success is not limited to a heartwarming experience. The moment of calling is just the beginning. The depth of success is bound up in our faithfulness to the talents that God gives us. We must learn faithfully everything that we can in the areas of our gifting, our crafts. Additionally, we must use them every opportunity we get. This is part of the development process.

Study and practice. You will unearth the potential for success that is bundled in the depths of your talent. If you play basketball, study Michael Jordan and others who are pros. Go to the gym and practice.

If you are a singer, study Luciano Pavarotti, Celine Dion, Donny Hathaway, Frank Sinatra, Aretha Franklin, Shirley Caesar, Sam Cooke, and other pros. Sing in the shower, in the backyard, at small talent shows, etc.

If you are a preacher, study Bishop T. D. Jakes, Rev. Dr. E. Stanley Jones, Rev. Dr. Charles Stanley, Rev. Dr. Gardner C. Taylor, Rev. Dr. Samuel Dewitt Proctor, Rev. Dr. Teresa Fry Brown, Rev. Dr. Elizabeth Brown Taylor, Rev. Dr. Carolyn Knight, and others. Study them to develop your own gifts, not to imitate them. Then, practice your skills with you're your family, friends, and neighbors.

In other words, don't just put that gift on the shelf and look at it. It does you and others more good when you maximize its potential. Do everything you can to make the most of it. We flourish best along the trajectory of our own gifting.

Productivity as Faithfulness

In Matthew 25:14-30, Jesus shares the illustrious parable on Talents. Along with the profound theological point as pertaining to the nature of talents and the Kingdom of God, you will note His outlook on the issue of faithfulness. Matthew 25:15-23 states,

To one he gave five talents, to another two, to another one, to each according to his ability. Then he went away. He who had received the five talents went at once and traded with them, and he made five talents more. So also he who had the two talents made two talents more. But he who had received the one talent went and dug in the ground and hid his master's money. Now after a long time the master of those servants came and settled accounts with them. And he who had received the five talents came forward, bringing five talents more, saying, 'Master, you delivered to me five talents; here I have made five talents more.' His master said to him, *'Well done, good and faithful servant.* You have been faithful over a little; I will set you over much. Enter into the joy of your master.' And he also who had the two talents came forward, saying, 'Master, you delivered to me two talents; here I have made two talents more.' His master said to him, *'Well done, good and faithful servant.'* (emphasis mine)

Jesus' view on faithfulness means more than what we often think of when referring to the term. We are not faithful because we ostentatiously hold a position. Faithfulness does not mean simply to hold on to what God has given to us. This parable teaches us that faithfulness has to do with intentional multiplication. Some people think that to be faithful means to be task-oriented. So, they work all the time and appear faithful to a task.

The salient question is this: "How have I multiplied with what God has given to me?" A depth of faithfulness implied in Jesus' parable has to do with productivity. It takes a person who has a positively-thinking and creative mind, one who has business savvy to multiply. Beyond the movies, no one waves a magic wand and sees productivity appear. Success does not just happen. Believe it or not, we were born with the equipment necessary to succeed, yet situations in life intimidate some of us. As a result, we may never activate our innate ability for productivity. So, we mark time by going in circles, incubating our talents rather than productively using them.

There is more to Jesus' Parable of the Talents. A third person was assigned a talent and did nothing to multiply it. Perhaps, like many of us, he was intimidated because his friends had more to work with than he did. So, he decided that his one talent was not worth trying to multiply. Fear gripped his heart. Like many of us, he didn't have the courage to step out with a little bit. Matthew 25:24-27 explains what Jesus thought of this:

> The third also who had received the one talent came forward, saying, 'Master, I knew you to be a hard man, reaping where you did not sow, and gathering where you scattered no seed, so I was afraid, and I went and hid your talent in the ground. Here you have what is yours.' But his master answered him, *'You wicked and slothful servant!* ...you ought to have invested my money with the bankers, and at my coming I should have received what was my own with interest.

Quite explicitly, Jesus associates faithfulness with multiplication. Importantly, however, Jesus' emphasis is not so much on financial multiplication. He more specifically emphasizes the multiplying of treasures, time, and talents through wise investments. God gives us so many different talents and with different proportions. Some of us are given a few, and others are given many. Some talents are rare, and others are more commonplace. We are often tempted to be jealous of the popular talents or the people with many talents. Yet, God does not waste one talent. Each of us has at least one talent. God gives talents with purpose assigned to each of them.

Our success depends on how we invest that which God gives to us. It is imperative that we take that talent or those talents—whatever they are—and value them enough to apply our hearts and minds to their productivity. We can measure our faithfulness to God by how we use the talents that He has given to us.

Significantly, moreover, we must not evaluate the fullness of our fruitfulness solely based on the bottom line, financially speaking. God freely gives us time as long as we live. Treasures (of finances) follow vision, but God has orchestrated our lives so that the matter of choosing what we would do with our talents is in our courts. What will we do with them? While we need to apply our time and treasures wisely, their value depends on how we apply our talents. In other words, we must align our time and treasures with our talents. We become productive when we use our God-given time, treasures and talents faithfully.

Not Just the Numbers

Biblical faithfulness includes more than generating numbers. It involves holistic human flourishing. Jesus invites us to flourish *in* Him. There is no better way to flourish than in the One who died to give eternal life to us. John 15:5b records Jesus saying, "Whoever abides in me and I in him, he it is that bears much fruit, for apart from me you can do nothing." While we remain faithful to God's Word, grounded in Christ-centered virtue (Christian character traits), we will also progress in God's purpose for us. Inspired by Jesus' words in John 15:5b, the legendary Gospel singer, Mahalia Jackson, penned the song lyrics,

> Without God, I could do nothing, Oh Lord; Without God, You know all my life would fail; Without God, My life would be rugged, Oh Lord; Yes, Just like a ship, Without a sail.

Succinctly stated, faithfulness to Christ cultivates our holistic fruitfulness. Stated differently, the strength, compass, and goals to accomplish life's meaningful fulfillment are made possible only as a byproduct of our loyalty to Christ. Aristotle explains success in philosophical terms, but only Jesus Christ can realize the human longing for true success.

Moreover, in the pages ahead, I wish to locate my discussion on the pathway to achievement—more specifically, within the framework of Christian success: that is, Christ first. On this basis, these principles are valuable keys to unlock many doors of achievement: college degrees, jobs, businesses, ministries, and more.

It is important to note, moreover, that Christ-centered success is characterized by the need to help others rather than merely to attain desirable ends for self-aggrandizement. As Jesus poured out himself for humankind, His disciples are also called to self-pour on the behalf of others. Paul notes that through Christ's self-pouring approach God highly exalted Him and made His name great. In Philippians 2:6–9, Paul explains,

> Though he (Jesus) was in the form of God, did not count equality with God a thing to be grasped, but emptied himself, by taking the form of a servant, being born in the likeness of men. And being found in human form, he humbled himself by becoming obedient to the point of death, even death on a cross. Therefore, God has highly exalted him and bestowed on him the name that is above every name.

Moreover, in as much as Christ's victory is explained in Paul's letter to the Philippians as the outcome of self-emptying, we must discover a God-kind of success through sacrificing ourselves for others.

The Test of True Ambition

Like many others, I have always dreamed of success. The concept of achievement has had various meanings throughout the seasons of my life. As a small child, I saw adults as the epitome of success. My greatest ambition was to grow-up. "If only I could be like the adults in the living room with my parents," I thought when our parents would send my siblings and me to the back room when company came over to the house. At that time, attainment was attached to age.

Then, I went to a parochial school. Starting in the fourth grade, I read books about missionaries and discovered new realms of success, learning about the important work that missionaries were doing for Christ: feeding the hungry, translating Bibles, building orphanages, and faith-sharing in unreached areas of the world that had not heard the gospel that touched my life. I was, particularly, fascinated with Hudson Taylor's evangelism in China and Rochunga Pudite's arduous journey through the jungles of India to pursue his education. Later, he would sponsor Bible translations into multiple languages, become a leader of Bible colleges, and preach the gospel throughout the world. These stories and others struck me as powerful. As an impressionable kid, I processed their success as restricted to the works they did. So, I wanted to be like them!

Over the years, I have come to realize that a God-kind of success has to do with the pursuit of one's own God-given purpose. When we see others who we consider successful, many of us may be tempted to wish we were them or to want to be like them. But, success is not the measure of another person's experience. Success is tapping into what God has designed each person to become. Rick Warren said it well:

> There is a God who made you for a reason, and your life has profound meaning! We discover that meaning and purpose only when we make God the reference point of our lives.[10]

In other words, one person can't successfully fulfill another person's purpose. Each of us has to achieve being the best that we can be. Whether we are called to pursue law, medicine, custodial services, engineering, the ministry, secretarial services, business, education, or something else, true success is found in the primary pursuit of Christ and the secondary pursuit of Christ-like service to others.

God Gives Talent; Give Success to God

Who is the person that God created me to be? How can I become the best at that? Self-discovery only happens as we discern and learn who Christ is. He is God incarnate. Through discovering God, we discover who God wants us to become. Along with the gifts and talents He gives to us, God gives us passions and intense interests. Our job is to channel those assets in a way that brings glory to God. We start that process by orienting our souls towards Him, fixing our minds on Him, and working hard to please Him. When we attain that success, we give it to him through our testimony that it is the Lord's doing. We set the Lord as our priority from beginning of the journey and never lose sight of Him. With Christ-centered character-traits as building blocks or as steps on the road to success, we remain grounded in Christ, giving Him the glory every step of the way.

In this book, we will explore seven key ingredients for character building. Also, I will offer what I hope to be words of challenge, inspiration, and motivation. I will share part of my own journey and some of my family's testimonies in hopes that they will encourage you, the reader, in your journey toward success. By God's grace, success belongs to each of us. When each person understands and pursues success, we all will experience it.

Regardless of the vicissitudes of life, your help is in the name of the Lord. I hope that by the time you finish reading this short book you will be fully persuaded that, with G on your side, you can do what God has called you to do. Trust God, and go for it!

1. D. Arcelious Harris, Facebook Post, March 9, 2014.

2. Stephen R. Covey, *The Seven Habits of Highly Effective People* (New York: Simon and Schuster, 1989), 122–123.

3. Tom Morris, *True Success: A New Philosophy of Excellence* (New York: Berkley Books, 1994).

4. Ibid.

5. Ibid, 34.

6. Lori Sharn, "Mother Teresa dies at 87." No pages. Online source: http://usatoday30.usatoday.com/news/mothert/mother01.htm (Accessed February 19, 2014).

7. B. Courtney McBath, *Living @ the Next Level* (New York: Simon & Schuster, 2008), 189.

8. Aristotle, *Nicomachean Ethics*, trans. by W. D. Ross, Book I, Chapter 4. No page numbers: Online source. http://classics.mit.edu/Aristotle/nicomachaen.1.i.html (Accessed February 18, 14). Also see Chapter 5–12 for more discussion of happiness and good as the goal of human life.

9. Ruth Haley Barton, *Strengthening the Soul of Your Leadership: Seeking God in the Crucible of Ministry* (Downers Grove, IL: IVP Books, 2008), 74.

Warren, *The Purpose Driven Life: What On Earth Am I Here for?* apids, MI: Zondervan, 2002), 25.

1

GO IN FAITH!

Lord, I'm going to hold steady on to You and
You've got to see me through.

—Harriet Tubman

LIFE TEACHES US that the road to success is not always easy. To borrow from the African-American anthem, written by James Weldon Johnson, "Lift Every Voice and Sing,"

> Stony the road we trod,
> Bitter the chastening rod,
> Felt in the days when hope unborn had died;
> Yet with a steady beat,
> Have not our weary feet
> Come to the place for which our fathers sighed?
> We have come over a way that with tears has
>   been watered,
> We have come, treading our path through the
>   blood of the slaughtered,
> Out from the gloomy past,
> Till now we stand at last
> Where the white gleam of our bright star is cast.

The African-American historical experience teaches us that trouble is not permanent. Faith helps us to overcome the most difficult challenges. Another songwriter, Albert Goodson, wrote, "We've Come This Far by Faith." This song has become somewhat of a sacred song in African-American Christian circles, certainly in our household while we were growing up. The first verse to Goodson's song is this:

> Don't be discouraged with troubles in your life;
> He'll bear your burdens and move all [misery]
>   and strife.

I am not one to say that God makes hardships happen to make us stronger. However, I am convinced that God knows how to take chaos that happens in our lives and produce a beautiful outcome. Yet, we must participate in the process. God does the work, and we simply hold on to faith.

Success is birthed through hardships and often through overwhelming chaos. Unfortunately, some people abandon success, unknowingly. Fear can terminate success. Many of us become afraid to endure the intensity of labor that success requires. Others simply fail to understand the relationship between faith and progress. Faith makes the difference between failure and success! Faith is powerful in the face of challenges.

Movie producer, DeVon Franklin, wrote a book titled, *Produced by Faith*. He points out,

> If career is shaping who you become, and your faith isn't integrally involved in your career choices, then what good is your faith? It's time to start looking at your faith not as an obstacle to

> your career progress, but as an asset … It's time
> to unify faith and career as dual assets toward
> achieving the same goal … Career should be a
> spiritual pursuit, not just a physical or financial
> one.[1]

In essence, faith is the compass to find the purpose that God has created us for. We can't afford to lose faith. We must feed our faith and starve our doubts. Christ-centered success requires that our faith remains steadfast in the face of challenges.

In Luke 22:31ff, Jesus is about to be crucified. Peter has the right heart to maintain loyalty to Christ no matter what. Certainly, God has chosen Peter for greatness. He would become the chief apostle to the Jews someday. It would be soon but just not at the moment. In fact, knowing how difficult the road ahead would become, Jesus has a chat with Peter and warns him that Satan wants to sift him like wheat falling through the holes of an old-fashioned sifter. Jesus says to Peter that His only prayer for him is that his "faith may not fail" (Luke 22:31-32). He would need the strength that faith brings when fear grips his heart.

Often, people think of faith as some opiate to help us cope with life. It does help us to live better, but we must realize that faith is practical. Those who experience the power of faith testify that faith works. In other words, as with Peter, faith is essential for conquering the inevitable challenges along the path of success.

Faith is creative. It makes a way where there is no way. Existence as we know it was birthed through faith. Hebrews 11:3 states, "By faith we understand that the world was created by the word of God, so that what is seen was made out of things which do not appear." When we live a life of faith, positive things happen that would not otherwise happen. Opportunities come, seemingly, out of nowhere.

Trust God

The Greek word for faith is *pistis*. A theological meaning of *pistis* denotes divine persuasion. This means that God initiates true faith, yet we have a responsibility in the matter. God compels, and we surrender; we agree with God. The forces of life compete with the compelling nature of God. Situations and circumstances say, "No," but God says, "Yes." Or, God says, "No," but situations and circumstances say, "Yes." Often times, we find ourselves between the contrariness to God that infiltrates life and the Word of God. We must trust God no matter what. We must believe God in spite of what we see and experience in life. Christ-centered success is a journey of reliance on God.

On Christ, the Solid Rock, I Stand!

Another way to think about being faithful (other than how I have discussed it in the Introduction) is to be "full of faith." I think of faith in two major ways: as a noun and as a verb. As a noun, "faith" can be used interchangeably with the term, "religion," as in Christianity, Islam, and Buddhism. These are often called *Faiths*.

In addition, *faith* can be used as a verb, as in the belief that something will happen. Have you ever said, "I have faith that things will work out"? In other words, we don't know how it will work out, but we trust God that it will. Often, we hear people say, "I am going to do this or that by faith." They are saying that though they don't know the details of how they will do it, they are convinced that it will work out somehow because God said it. To be full of faith, we need both: faith as noun and as verb!

My Faith Grounds Me

I am grateful to have been born into a devout Christian family with parents who instilled the value of the faith (as a noun) in me as a young child. It is important that we believe God just as much as we believe what God is able to do for us or give to us. Therefore, being a Christian is important on this journey. There will be times when God is all we have. We will discover that success really depends on God.

Sometimes, our worlds seem to crumble, and it happens so suddenly and unexpectedly. It feels somewhat like a whiplash. You don't have time to brace yourself for the impact because you don't see it coming. Of all the people you have encouraged and helped over the years, sometimes there seems to be no one to help and to give the support you need. Where do we go? In the words of that famous song from R & B sensation, Xscape, "Who Can I Run To?" During those inevitable moments of disappointment and ambivalence—when deals fall through, people walk away, life seems to crumble, and our ambitions seem to hang in the balance—we need *faith* as a noun.

Faith is the only constant when all else fails. Faith becomes a refuge of consolation. Faith brings answers to the tough questions of the soul. In the Psalms, David acknowledges the need for faith as a noun:

> From the end of the earth I call to you when my
>   heart is faint.
> Lead me to the rock that is higher than I,
> for you have been my refuge, a strong tower.
> (Ps. 61:2–3a)

When our feet grow weary, when we encounter unexpected turbulence, or when our hearts are heavy with ambivalence, David is teaching us to trust who God is more than what God can do. It's when we can't see our way and when we don't have a word from God on the matter that faith becomes our foundation. That is *faith* as a noun!

My Faith: A Faith that I Can Feel Sometimes

My personal relationship with the Lord is important to every aspect of my life. As a young church boy, my family not only went to church but also prayed together at home. As far back as I can remember, I have had an awareness of God. My first experience with God, however, was when I was five years old. I was singing in the children's choir one Wednesday night at church. My mom was the director and taught us the song, "Stop by Jesus; Stop by. We need the Lord to stop by." I was the song leader of this upbeat song. By midway the song, I was dancing! The experience of God was real for me. Later that night, my brother and friend poked fun at me. However, my mom and Sister Eloise Childs, one of the mothers of the church, encouraged me and affirmed my experience as the movement of the Holy Spirit upon me. As you could imagine, as a young and impressionable five-year-old, that experience confirmed that

God was real and the Holy Spirit could touch me in a real way.

My spiritual formation began at this early age. That experience with God as I sang "Stop by Jesus" was foundational for my journey of faith. I have learned to trust the God of that experience. The experience sparked something in me; it has never left my memory. I knew that I had encountered God in a profound way. I was sure that God was real, and that assuredness has guided my life until now.

Even now, in my mind's eye, I can see my little self in front of the church with my siblings and friends experiencing the movement of God. There is something profound about exposing children to the move of God. Even as adults, it is equally important to learn the value of faith formation. Being exposed to faith from a very young age helped me to understand the importance of God-related things. Upon this faith, I have been able to build my life.

The proverb worked for me: "Train up a child in the way he should go; even when he is old he will not depart from it" (Proverbs 22:6). Stated another way in The Message Bible, "Point your kids in the right direction—when they're old they will not be lost." When children are exposed to faith early, they grow up with a foundation of faith upon which they can build the rest of their life, a platform that "without God, we can do nothing" (see John 15:5). That platform of faith easily becomes the all-inclusive platform for both religious life and career pursuit. God becomes central not only in Church but also in work and play. We learn to pray about everything, believing that if "it" is going to happen for us, "it" can only happen because God is at the foundational level of making "it" happen for us.

Believe God No Matter What

The second way of thinking about faith toward a tangible goal has to do with a hope in God for a particular thing. When we want something, we not only consult God, but we believe God for it. In this way, faith not only grounds us, but it also propels us forward. Proverbs 3:5–6 says,

> Trust in the Lord with all your heart,
> and do not lean on your own understanding.
> In all your ways acknowledge him,
> and he will make straight your paths.

The Hebrew word used for "trust" is *batach,* which originates in the term "refuge." This means that we can depend safely and solely on the Lord for success. When we do, he will *yashar 'orach,* which translates as "make our road prosperous." Trusting God with our whole heart is the type of faith that we need to attain holistic success.

Abraham provides a great example of what it means to fully trust God for success, not knowing the details. When he was 75 years old, God told him to leave Haran, and Abraham had no idea where he would go. He could have used excuses not to obey, excuses such as, "I'm too old"; or, "I have already built my life here in Ur"; or, "I don't mind the change, but I need more details." None of these justifiable concerns seemed to dissuade Abraham from the path onto which God called him. This is particularly interesting because Abraham's parents did not raise him in a monotheistic religion. He discovered who God is on his own, and he learned to trust God by himself. His faith (as a noun) taught him to trust God even when God gave him the oddest instructions.

Several times, Abraham's faith called for him to do things that seemed strange to the human mind. He learned to simply obey God. Sometimes, I find this hard to do, but Abraham continues to teach me that we cannot know the good things that God has in store until we simply obey Him. Abraham could not have known the importance of the legacy that he would leave until this day. As a result of his obedience, Jesus Christ is called the seed of Abraham!

Seed of Abraham? Sarah was barren. But, God said that she would have a child. This was the most confusing promise of God that Abraham seemed to have ever heard, yet the God of nature defied nature and gave Sarah a son in her old age. His name was Isaac. The name Isaac means, "Son of my laughter." His name marks the moment that Sarah laughed when the angel of the Lord broke the news that she would birth a son.

The lesson here is that, sometimes, God will say things that are downright laughable. There is no human way possible that that thing could happen. Yet, God has a way of leaving the experts scratching their heads and asking, "What in the world? How in the world?"

Relating the story of Abraham to this issue of success, faith makes success possible in the face of what sometimes appears to be impossible. We need the substance of faith that endures challenges, which will certainly come our way. The writer of Hebrews says, "Now faith is the assurance of things hoped for, the conviction of things not seen" (Heb. 11:1)

During tough times (and there have been many), it is the childhood experience with God mentioned above that produces faith in me. I met God through a religious experience, and that experience taught me that God is near me. My parents taught me, and the scriptures suggest that if I hold tightly to God, He will carry me through life's ups and downs. Borrowing a prayer from Harriet Tubman, "Lord, I'm going to hold steady on to You and You've got to see me through."

In this way, *faith* also becomes a verb. In other words, when the vicissitudes of life challenge what God has for us, we have to "faith" our way through. Note that the confidence of faith is not reliance merely on a "desired thing," "an ambition," or "the goal;" rather, it is full confidence in God—who God is and what God says—to see us through any struggle. When we are able to grasp hold of this principle, the stresses that are often associated with the pursuit of success lessen.

If you are like me, you yearn for a stress-less life. But, you also don't want to appear lazy or lackadaisical. You want to be productive without the stress. Well, stress-less faith does just that for us. It energizes us to keep moving without worrying. Matthew 1:23 recalls that, just before Jesus' birth, the angel said to Joseph, "Behold, the virgin [Mary] shall conceive and bear a son, and they shall call his name Immanuel" (which means, God with us). When we grab hold of the depth of faith in what it means for God in Christ to be with us, we will gain authority over worry. Challenges become stepping stones rather than cases for worry. As we step upon the stones, we elevate higher than stress.

Now, I know that you may be thinking, "It's easier to say this than to live it." Believe me; I am with you. Yet, I have learned that when we learn to let go of self-reliance to trust God, life is so much better. Oh, how I yearn for this depth of faith in every aspect of my life. Lord, help me in my seasons of unbelief!

A Little Faith Can Do Big Things

It has been said that we can know how many seeds are in an apple, but we can't know how many apples are in a seed. We would need to plant the apple seed and wait a season. In due time, there will be more apples than we could have imagined. The point is that a little seed can do more than it appears. Jesus said that if we have faith the size of a grain of mustard seed, we are empowered by even such a small dosage of faith to move mountains (Matthew 17:20). In other words, when we have faith, we can do big things!

Often, we think that if we have financial resources, we can do big things, but success can't be bought with money. It is birthed from within. As strange as it seems, faith attracts resources.

A pastor-friend shared with me that God gave him a vision to build a ministry. He knew that he did not have the resources on his own. So, he was renting space from another church. Then, he moved into a local hotel ballroom. After about two years, the Lord put on his heart that it was time for him to get his own building. His dilemma was that he did not have adequate financial resources to make that step.

The beauty of my friend's story was that, when he decided to just obey God and look for a building, the money started to pour in. Someone approached him and gave him a $10,000 check! In the words of the saying from the old church, "If you make one step, He (God) will make two. There is no limit to what God can do." If we can just believe despite the odds, in due time, the seed of faith will produce a harvest.

Christian faith begins with God and must translate into practice, the way we look at and deal with life's situations. The operative word here is "courage." We must seek to remain encouraged. Read encouraging books. Listen to encouraging sermons. Hang around encouraging people. Constructive encouragement is essential to success. When we are discouraged, we begin to lose. Discouragement is the enemy of success.

Recently, I came across an interesting article on MindReality.com, which was written by its founder, Enoch Tan. The article was titled, "The Measure of Faith is the Measure of Success."[2] Tan has some valuable insights about the strength of courage and what it means to live by faith. Tan explains that discouragement drains us such that anything we imagine to do becomes unreachable. We lose energy when we are discouraged. In fact, the loss of courage diminishes even those savvy moves that we would make instinctively when the courage level is high. In this vein, Tan rightly notes,

> Courage is the leader in the mental realm, and when it is down all other faculties do down as well. What most people in great failure need is to have their courage restored, renewed.[3]

Courage is the engine of faith. It is what the Psalmist meant when he said,

I would have lost heart, unless I had believed
That I would see the goodness of the L<small>ORD</small>
In the land of the living.
(Ps. 27:13, NKJV, emphasis mine)

A small amount of faith that is able to do big things is defined by courage to continue believing. No other virtue will produce success if the core tenet of faith is absent.

You May See the Glory, But You Don't Know the Story

There are many testimonies about how faith works things out mysteriously. I have mentioned several of them in different sections of this book. Dr. Emory Alexander, a successful orthopedic surgeon in Columbus, Georgia, once spoke at a graduation ceremony. He pointed out that his own journey as a successful surgeon has been paved with ups and downs. Before the honor of operating on movie stars and NFL players, Alexander was a struggling medical student. He commented that we see people's success, but we don't know that there were many failures on the road to success.

Similarly, Nigerian pastor and entrepreneur, Rev. Moses Onodua, points out that the success stories of billionaires are often filled with disadvantages. In his book, *Success in Business,* Rev. Onodua explains how many people who are not successful in life offer excuses for not succeeding. According to Rev. Onodua's assessment, most often, they point fingers at others instead of looking inward for the reasons for their seemingly low-level life. Rev. Onodua advises such persons to jettison that mindset and think positively about people that have "made it" despite their disadvantages.[4]

We must step up to the plate. As I mentioned in the Introduction, we must take responsibility for our own success, but we also must own up to our failures. In general, the ones who make it are those who have the faith to flip failures into something positive. I often say, "You may see the glory, but you don't know the story." The glory is the goal, the public image of success. The story usually feels like it is never going to end, sometimes like a never-ending, bad movie or a horror story. It is often packed with private frustration and filled with cloudy days and with long nights. In the midst of it all, faith produces glory out of a less-than-favorable story.

Rest in God; Faith Works in Patience

There have been times when I *say* that I believe God to work things out for me. Perhaps, I say it because I know it is the right thing to say, but when I drill down, I realize that I really live by more doubt than faith. Faith is tough! When the man brought his son to Jesus to be cured from the demons that tortured him, it's no wonder that he asked for help in the area of faith. In Mark's account of the story, he reports,

> And Jesus said to him [the possessed boy's father], "'If you can [cure your son]!' All things are possible for one who believes." Immediately the father of the child cried out and said, "I believe; help my unbelief!' (Mark 9:23–24)

Many times, the stress of a situation overworks our minds and bodies to the point where we don't know whether we believe or not. Growing up, they would say, "Sometimes, we don't know whether we are going or coming." But, that's reality for people who live under so much stress from doing and going all the time. In the story above, the demons not only tormented the child but also stressed out the father so much so that he needed relief just as much as his son — only, in a different way. The father needed relief from doubt. So, in the same request for help for his son, he seemed to say, "While I need you to help my son, please help me to have more faith." Doubt can hurt us. It overworks our hearts and minds from the stress that it brings. We need rest from the stress!

In *Holy Spirit, Holy Living*, I explain that *rest* is a godly virtue. Ambitious people often work, work, work! Working is important and is necessary to achieving our goals. As they say, "If we don't work, we won't eat." At the same time, we must not allow work to overwhelm us to the point that we don't know whether we are living by faith or in doubt. Some people work so hard that they think the sum total of their success depends on how much or how hard they work — these are often obsessive-compulsive people and Type-A personalities. These people thrive on work. They find little time to rest, becoming like the man in the story above. They become caught in a trap between belief and unbelief.

The ambitious Christian must understand that rest is related to faith. When we are rested, we think more clearly. Also, when we rest in God, we can hear Him more clearly; we can depend on God better. Later, I will explain the relationship between faith and hearing. But, for now, I must assert, "Faith comes from hearing, and hearing through the word of Christ" (Romans 10:17). If we work all the time, we can't hear a word from God upon which to build our faith.

We must rest in God and listen to Him for our next steps on the road to success.

Also, there is an intricate connection between faith, rest, and patience. We have heard it said many times: "Patience is a virtue." As a virtue, patience teaches us that God may not come through when we think that He should, but when He does, He overwhelms us with the perfect timing. Patience keeps us in a mode of expectation. God wants us to expect that He will do what He said He is going to do. Hebrews 6:12 states,

> And we desire each of you to show... full assurance of hope until the end, so that you may not be sluggish, but imitators of those who through faith and patience inherit the promises.

We must position ourselves to receive from the Lord, not allowing situations and circumstances to control our sincere expectation.

In Time, God Will Open the Door(s)

When I was pursuing theological education, the process of getting in and finishing college and seminary seemed fine. The schoolwork was challenging—another story for a different book—but I knew what I wanted to do, and I had little trouble with the process. However, upon completion of seminary, it was hard for me to determine what I was going to do next. I had several well-wishers making suggestions that were great ideas, but I wanted to make the decision that was best for me.

I wanted to enroll in another graduate degree program. So, I applied to approximately six or seven graduate programs. The logic of applying to several schools was simple. The more schools I applied to, the more chances I had to secure my next educational success. However, in only a few weeks from applying, I started receiving letters of rejection in the mail. After a few, I was disappointed but not discouraged. However, as most of the schools sent letters declining my application, I grew discouraged. Many of my friends were excited about their next career steps. As we shared stories, I was embarrassed to let them know that I didn't know what I would be doing next. Yet, the more I prayed about it and the more I reflected on my options, the more convinced I became that pursuing further studies was what I was supposed to do. I did not want to pursue this direction out of spite or even jealousy. These vices are not righteous ingredients for long-term success.

I have learned, moreover, that success comes with a price. Sometimes, it is one that is hard to pay. Yet, we are called to pay the price of patience and endurance. Let's be sure that we pay it with a righteous rationale. Certainly, if this or that is God's will—as my brother, Alexander Harris, used to sing often—"He will make a way, somehow." However, *when* and *how* were the frustrating questions that haunted me for months.

During my season of prayer and seeking God, I attended church one Saturday. We had a time of prayer and intercession. The Spirit moved powerfully. There was a sense of divine expectancy that filled the church. We travailed in the Spirit for what seemed like hours—in a good way. With different interests—some of them were unspoken—we sought God for answers. Amidst the moving of the

Spirit, my Dad had a prophetic Word. He said, "The Lord said, go to the door, and it will open." I will never forget that moment. Indeed, this Word was for me, I thought.

But, how would this Word apply practically to my situation. I thought for the next day or so. Then, the following Monday, I decided to call Yale to see if they had received my application for the STM program. I really wanted this to be my door that would open. The voice on the other end was friendly with me. She said, "Hold on, Mr. Harris." Soon, she returned to the phone with great news. She said, "Congratulations, Mr. Harris. You have been accepted into the program." Indeed, the Word of the Lord was true! God opened my door!

In Judges 6, Israel was facing adversity from the Midianites and the Amalekites. They were crying out to the Lord for help. Gideon was beating wheat by the winepress for fear of his enemies.

The angel of the Lord met Gideon by a tree. Gideon was working hard to make ends meet, while also hiding from the enemy. The Lord assured Gideon that He had heard Israel's prayers and that help was on the way. Then, the Lord shocked Gideon when He told Gideon that Israel's blessing was in him. Gideon was praying with the people but did not know that the success of the nation was hidden inside him.

When God hears our prayers, we must not allow fear, inferiority, and low self-esteem to stifle our progress. Like Gideon, we need somebody to tell us that we have what it takes! Fear and inferiority often set up a petition between our current reality and destiny. Our future is waiting on us, and others will be blessed when we overcome fear and walk through the, sometimes, unexpected doors that God opens for us.

Coming from the small town of Manchester, Georgia, I could not have imagined actually hearing the words from Yale, "Congratulations, Mr. Harris. You have been accepted." I had only dreamed of going to Yale. As a young boy at Christian Way Academy, I read inspiring stories of men who attended Yale, such as Jonathan Edwards and David Brainard, which developed a deep desire in me to go there. At that stage of my life, I thought, "I only wish." In many ways, I did not feel "good enough." Subconsciously, I assumed that Yale was for "those people." In essence, God was saying to me, "No, Antipas. I have opened the door for you. You have what it takes. It's in you! Go with what you have. And, I will be with you to help you to succeed!"

I have learned that the true path of success is not the door that we wish would open. Success is on the inside, regardless of our disadvantaged situations, social status or geographical locale. The doors that God opens for us are opportunities. But, success is fueled from that thing on the inside that says, "I can do this." With faith and intense focus, we are to follow the paths of success through the doors that God opens for us.

If God Said So, Put Your Foot On It!

Faith makes wishes come true. Hebrews 11:1 teaches a lesson that I continue to learn over and over: "Now faith is the assurance of things hoped for, the conviction of things not seen." In other words, faith can make wishes come true. Yet, faith is not merely wishful thinking. Wishes must become prayers. Prayers must include both a petition to God and a Word from God on the issue.

Indeed, there is a connection between faith and God's Word. The Word of God is the essence of God. This is why Jesus is God. His incarnation was the Word made flesh in the world. German theologian, Karl Barth, once explained, "It is the Word, Christ, to whom faith refers because He presents Himself to it as its object, that makes faith faith, real experience."[5] I find Barth's wisdom to be helpful; our faith in God is only as real as our faith in God's Word, Jesus. Therefore, faith in Jesus is as authentic as our submission to God's Word.

This reminds me of two particular passages in the Old Testament, among many others. First, not long before he died, Moses shared these words with Israel:

> The Lord will make you the head and not the tail, and you shall only go up and not down, if you obey the commandments of the Lord your God … being careful to do them. (Deut. 28:13)

Although Moses would not live much longer and would not even make it to the Promised Land with them, he was confident that God's promises are tied to God's Word. If God said it, it would happen. The only condition was to hold fast to what God says.

The second passage that comes to mind is from a conversation between Joshua and God, just after Moses died. God had a plan for Joshua. He chose Joshua to lead Israel into the promises that God had waiting for them. What an awesome yet daunting responsibility! Naturally, Joshua was concerned about his own competence to lead God's people successfully. In prayer, God spoke to Joshua concerning the relationship between faith, God's Word, and success. In part, God says,

> Only be strong and very courageous, being careful to do according to all the law that Moses my servant commanded you. Do not turn from it to the right hand or to the left, that you may have *good success* wherever you go. This Book of the Law shall not depart from your mouth, but you shall meditate on it day and night, so that you may be careful to do according to all that is written in it. For then you will make your way prosperous, and then you will have *good success.* (Josh. 1:7b–8, emphasis mine)

The message is clear. God's Word is the foundation for "good success!" Before we plunge ahead, we must seek the wisdom of God's Word. As we plunge ahead, we must remain faithful to God's Word. The journey of "good success" requires that we remain attuned to God's Word because, in the Word, we find God's Will for our lives. God knows the end from the beginning. His Word will not fail! If God's Word reveals a thing, we can put our foot on it, knowing that it's the right thing to do, the right way to go, and the right way to do it. The question becomes, is there a Word from the Lord?

In the New Testament, Paul explains the necessity of hearing a Word from the Lord. He says, "So faith comes from hearing, and hearing through the word of Christ" (Romans 10:17). This means that faith is not faith without a Word from God on which to build faith. Many of us don't even try because we live with so many imagined (or real) glass ceilings, looking at the sky but feeling like we can't breakthrough. In these situations, we don't pray believing that it's possible, or we tell God what we want but don't listen for His instructions upon which we can build our faith to achieve it. We incapacitate our own chances. When God says, "Go to the door. The door will open," we can approach the door with confidence in His Word. God's Word will not fail. So, we must submit our wishes and dreams to God and adhere to His Word. As the saints at our church used to say, "God will make a way where there is no way." When God says, "It is so," He will move heaven and earth to make our dreams come true. As they say, "If God said it, put your foot on it." We can trust God's Word!

---

1. DeVon Franklin, *Produced by Faith: Enjoy Real Success without Losing Your True Self* (New York: Simon & Schuster, 2011), 4.

2. I am hesitant to agree with Tan completely because he seems inclined to mingle the issue of human consciousness with the Ultimate Being, God, a bit more than I agree. Indeed, there is strength in consciousness. A mind that is submitted to God is more powerful than the consciousness, itself. Yet, a conscious courage to live out God's plan for one's life is a valuable virtue, a foundational principle for Christian success.

3. Enoch Tan, "The Measure of Faith is the Measure of Success." Nopage numbers. Online source. http://www.mindreality.com/the-measure-of-faith-is-the-measure-of-success (accessed April 5, 2014).

4. Moses Onodua, *Success in Business: A Systematic Approach to Business Survival* (Edo State, Nigeria: Freedom Publications, 2013), 83–84.

5. Karl Barth, *Church Dogmatics I, 1: The Doctrine of the Word of God*. Edited by G. W. Bromiley and T.F. Torrance (Edinburgh: T. & T. Clark, 2004), 230.

2

NO SUCCESS WITHOUT A VISION

*All successful people, men and women, are big
dreamers. They imagine what their future could be,
ideal in every respect, and then they work every day
toward their distant vision, that goal or purpose.*

—Brian Tracy

VISIONS ARE NOT MERELY GOOD IDEAS; they are God's ideas
that are spiritually revealed to us not only through words
but also through visions. Visions are spiritual experiences.
The Holy Spirit reveals to us our purpose by design. Spiritual experiences might be in the form of a trance but not
always. The Holy Spirit can reveal God's will for our lives
through a quickening of passion, an experience, or a
thought. Either way, success is born out of an awakening of
consciousness to our life's purpose. Many people overlook
this type of spiritual experience or brush it off as just an idea.
But, we know that God's in it when we try to move on, but
it just won't go away. Some people think they are just "fleeting thoughts," but they are really connected to passion. We
can't stop thinking about it. It is always in the back of our
minds even when we try to dismiss it.

It is prudent to ask, in the words of Paul on the road to Damascus, "What shall I do, Lord?" (Acts 22:10) Then, sit in the silence and listen for God's answer. Concerning the spiritual value of silence, Mother Teresa once said,

> We need to find God, and he cannot be found in noise and restlessness. God is the friend of silence. See how nature–trees, flowers, grass–grows in silence; see the stars, the moon and the sun, how they move in silence.[1]

Indeed, God reveals Himself to us profoundly through what we see. At the same time, God shows to us our purpose by design as we sit in the silence and listen. Mother Teresa explains, "And this silence, this listening, and this speaking to God, is prayer."[2]

Importantly, God breaks the silence with a question: "What do you see?" In this chapter, I will explore God-given, Spirit-revealed vision to help you discover its importance in charting the course for success.

Getting through the Fog

After God shows us His will, inevitably, there will be seasons when our vision is blurred. Have you ever been driving down the road and fog began to cover your windshield? It is hard to see where you are driving in the fog.

Do you ever find yourself seeking other people's approval? Or, do you feel that your success is crippled because someone doesn't recognize you or create a platform for your interests? Do you know anyone who looks to others to say who or what they should become?

Well, I admit that I have been that person. There are probably places in each of our lives or times in our lives when we have been that person. Indeed, we are created for community, but we are not created to gain our self-worth from someone else. If we are not careful, depending on others for self-worth will create fog in our lives.

Sometimes, it takes a while to fight through fog to gain clear vision. It is even prudent, at times, to pull the car over and wait a while. Pressing forward in thick fog can cause an accident.

Sometimes, on the road of life, we need to pause and just wait a while. In fact, I don't think that our westernized culture of instant gratification teaches us well concerning the value of waiting. It is a tragedy to speed down a particular path with no clear vision. In those times, we end up creating greater problems than necessary. In the fog, when our vision is blurred, patience is a virtue. Just pray, and wait on the Lord. He will reveal clarity of vision in due time.

In many cases, people and situations can create the fog. For example, other people's opinions can confuse us, particularly when they come from people we care about. When we are not in touch with our purpose by design, we can lose ourselves in other people's constant and well-meaning advice. We should listen to others for wisdom and guidance, yet we must remember that self-worth comes from within. This is why it's so important for each of us to surrender to God for clarity of vision. Then, we should invite others to rally around our clear visions to support and encourage us. I will say more about the important and appropriate role that others must play in our journey toward success in the chapter on "Connections."

Name the Somewhere!

Vision is not about the resources at our immediate disposal. Vision is all about what we don't have, what is beyond our immediate reach. In other words, vision is about where we are going. When we move past the fog, or even before the fog, the question on the issue of vision becomes this: "Do we know where we are going?"

Not long ago, Bishop T.D. Jakes lectured in my homiletics class at Regent University School of Divinity. At the end of his visit, Bishop Jakes and I went to lunch. He caught me off guard when seemingly out of nowhere he asked me, "Where are you going?" As intelligent as I wish I were, I found myself "at a loss of words." I was not expecting that question. I was also taken aback by the phrasing of the question.

What was the bishop really asking? Usually when someone asks, "Where are you going?" there is an understanding that a journey is involved. Was he confused? Did he think that I was literally heading somewhere? Did he think that I was planning to leave my post on the university's faculty? Or, was I missing something? Did he know something that I didn't know? Did I somehow mislead him to think that I was on a journey someplace soon? These questions flew through my mind in only a few seconds. I responded, "Me? What do you mean?"

He responded to me saying, "Yes, where are you going?"

Oh, I think I got it now! So, I asked, "Do you mean career wise?"

He said, "Yes, where are you going?"

I rattled off a few things but was rather vague. If he had asked me this a few years ago, I would have been much more focused and clearer in my response. In fact, there have been times when I was in conflict with family and friends that I would assert, "I do not have time for this. I am going *somewhere* with my life." Indeed, I knew what direction that I wanted to go. Yet, it occurred to me that life's busyness has a way of overshadowing that vision. We must take time out to ask ourselves again and again, "Where am I going?"

Several weeks after the meeting with Bishop Jakes, I continued to reflect on the question, "Where are you going?" Sometimes, we want someone else to tell us who we are. Or, perhaps, we can't name the somewhere because a search for affirmation has a tendency to hijack our life's purposes. So, in that moment, that question from the bishop was good for me in many ways. I discovered that, subconsciously, vision was giving way to increased focus on the minutia, the individual trees in the forest. The challenges that I have faced in recent years were weighing heavily on my confidence. Suddenly, I realized that what I saw so clearly as a vision for my life was being erased.

The paradox is that I am a leader by nature. Various gifts tests have confirmed this to be true. But, without confidence and clear direction, where was I going?

In different ways, we are all called to lead our own path to success. Yet, we can't lead if we don't know where we are going. Since this insight, I have continued to ask myself over and over, "Antipas, where are you going?" The more I ponder the question, the clearer the question becomes, the clearer the answer becomes, and the more confidence I regain.

When we are hardworking, it is easy to focus on the trees more than the forest. Stated more clearly, it becomes easy to get busy in the details and challenges of life such that we forget that where we are is not where we are going. The conversation with the bishop was sort of a wake-up call, reminding me to refocus on divine destiny.

I want to ask you the same question: "Where are you going?" Name the somewhere! Others may see your potential, but no one else can determine your destiny, and no one can get there for you. God puts it inside of us. Each of our destinies is up to us to discern.

In the Old Testament, the prophet, Habakkuk, records that he was complaining to God about the state of affairs around him. Habakkuk was begging for God to listen, to save, and to do something about the destruction and violence that he was seeing. God interrupted him:

> Write the vision; make it plain on tablets, so he may run who reads it. For still the vision awaits its appointed time; it hastens to the end—it will not lie. If it seems slow, wait for it; it will surely come; it will not delay. (Hab. 2:2-3)

In other words, God was saying, "Habakkuk. I know things are bad, but it is up to you to look inside and discern a better day ahead." But, what would it look like? Habakkuk was to envision that world and write down a concise statement on the destiny of his nation.

Aim at What You Name!

Life is a journey! It's our responsibility to choose what paths we will navigate. More importantly, we must know where we want to end up. Where does God want us to end up? Ask yourself, "Who has God created me to become?" When you think that you know, aim for it!

My formative days at Christian Way Academy helped me to understand what it means to "aim at what you name." The school used the Accelerated Christian Education Curriculum. There were no true "grade levels." Each student worked at her or his own pace. Of course, there were corresponding grade levels, based on the content comparison with the standards in the public schools. To stay on target, one would complete 12 "paces" in each subject per year. After all, we did not want to be in high school when our friends from the public schools were graduating. Moreover, to stay on target for graduation from high school at Christian Way Academy, at the start of the week, each student was required to set goals. We were to be realistic and not to feel hard-pressed to finish all 12 "paces," but if we could or even if we could finish more than 12 in each subject per year, that would be fine. The ACE curriculum is designed for either students who are slow learners or those who are fast learners.

The work that we did not complete, based on the goals we set, became our homework for that evening. This way, by the end of the week, we would have completed the weekly goals. A prudent student would calculate her or his weekly goals based on what it would take to finish those 12 "paces" in each subject by the end of the year and then work hard to reach the weekly goals to accomplish the vision to graduate on time.

Relating this scenario to "aiming at what you name," visions become dormant ideas when we fail to set goals to achieve them. It may surprise you for me to say that mere hard work does not achieve vision. Smart work achieves vision. By "smart work," I am talking about goal-setting and reaching those goals in a timely fashion.

Many people work hard for many years. In vernacular from the Deep South, "They work their fingers to the bones." Have you ever wondered why some people seem to work so hard but don't seem to have anything to show for it? A strong work ethic is an important ingredient to success. However, the missing ingredient is often clear vision. Morris points out,

> From the workplace to the world, many people seem to lack a vision… We can use the power of inner vision to structure our lives–our thoughts, actions, feelings, and attitudes. An inner vision gives guidance. An inner vision yields energy. An appropriate vision can enhance our lives.[3]

It has been said many times, "Work smarter, not harder." I am learning that living with a clear vision is a smart thing to do. It helps to eliminate over-working with poor results or unfavorable results. Morris further points out, "The power of an inner vision is healing, tranquility, new life, efficient direction, and real accomplishment."[4]

Many people, communities, businesses, and even churches can't seem to advance. They have the right gifts, talents, and connections to do great things. Yet, they give up, communities go awry, businesses close down, and churches die out. Some of them try the positive thinking strategies, prophesy success, do three laps, say, "It is mine in Jesus' name," pour oil in the corners, give more to charity, put a little more in the offering plate at church, and ask the accountability or Bible study group to bathe their situation in prayer. Yet, they can't seem to make ends meet. The more they do, the less they seem to accomplish. Again, to use a saying from the Deep South, "They can't win for losing."

Hard work without a clear vision compares to climbing up a hill to discover the bottom rather than the top. Stated another way in Scripture, "Where there is no vision, the people perish" (Proverbs 29:18a, KJV). For many years, I understood this passage as speaking to "other people" that might be affected by the lack of a vision. For example, the American people would perish if the president does not have a vision. But, in addition to this perspective, I now see this passage in a new light. An individual who lacks a vision for his or her own life would eventually short-circuit his or her own success.

Many of us not only work hard, but we wear ourselves out, resulting in poor physical, mental, and relational health. With all of the right moves and resources, those people can't seem to succeed. In such a case, their demise seems frustrating. One might ask, what is the problem? If someone has resources, how then does "the bottom fall out" (as it is said)? Are they cursed?

No! A crystallized vision can make a world of difference. My youngest brother, D. Arcelious, posted a thought-provoking comment on social media:

No one, man or woman, on this earth can stop the visions that I have seen of myself. People will disappoint you, mislead you, misuse you and often hurt you and hate on you. But the time is now to lose all inhibitions, shine forth and illuminate the path to success. [5]

Without a vision, many people experience the misfortune of having a wealth of talents, connections, and a strong work ethic with nothing to show for it. A young blogger from Ghana, Israelmore Ayivor, has commented,

The poorest person on earth is not the person who has no job, no cars, no money and no house. The poorest person is the one who has no vision. Visionlessness is poverty in disguise. [6]

As a result, so many opportunities pass them by—unexplored, unexamined, and overlooked—a sad memory of lost opportunity. In his book, *Understanding Your Potential*, Myles Monroe rightly points out,

The wealthiest spot on this plant is not the oil fields or Kuwait, Iraq, or Saudi Arabia. Neither is it the gold and diamond mines in South Africa, the uranium mines of Soviet Union, or the silver mines in Africa. Though it may surprise you, the richest deposits on our planet lie just a few blocks from our house. They rest in your local cemetery or graveyard. Buried beneath the soil within the walls of those sacred grounds are dreams that never came to pass... and purposes that were

never fulfilled. Our graveyards are filled with potential that remained potential. What a tragedy![7]

Everybody wants the best in life, but far too much talent
is wasted often where there is no clear focus. Say what you
see; name it; then, go for it!

You may say it is more complex than it sounds. But, the
real challenge and the real tragedy is that, many times, people never really know their own purpose. They never really
know their own potential. There are many discussions about
why this is the case, but there remains one foundational reason for it: they don't have insight into their God-ordained
purpose by design; thus, they never imagine a clear vision
for which they might align their resources to pursue. Once
we remove the smokescreen of excuses about limitations
and obstacles in life, we have to ask the question, "Do I really have a clear understanding about where God wants me
to go in life?"

Pause in the busyness and ask yourself with me in the
words of Bishop Jakes, "Where are you going?" If we want
to avoid the tragedy of graveyard wealth, we must pray to
God for a clear and concise vision and then set goals.

Pursue What You Aim at!

Drawing from the teachings of psychiatrist Viktor Frankl,
Stephen Covey points out, "The first and most basic habit of
a highly effective person in any environment [is] the habit of
proactivity."[8] Covey describes *proactivity* as more than
merely taking initiative. It means that, as human beings, we
are responsible for our own lives. He writes, "Our behavior
is a foundation of our decisions, not our [situations]… We

have the initiative and the responsibility to make things happen."[9] In other words, God makes our journey successful in so far as we are willing to take the steps forward in reaching the goals that we set to achieve the vision that we see.

The prophet Habakkuk was begging for God to listen, to save, and to do something about the destruction and violence that he constantly saw. God interrupted him:

> Write the vision; make it plain on tablets, so he may run who reads it. For still the vision awaits its appointed time; it hastens to the end—it will not lie. If it seems slow, wait for it; it will surely come; it will not delay. (Hab. 2:2-3)

In other words, if you want to see something different, you need to envision something different. Envisioning supersedes physical eyesight. It actually creates worlds that we can't see right now with physical eyes. The prophet is called to dig within himself and envision a better world.

Helen Keller was born both deaf and blind, yet she had vision. She once said, "The only thing worse than being blind is having no vision." Although she could not see with her physical eyes because she had no eyesight, she became the first deaf-blind person to earn a bachelor's of arts degree. She became proactive and achieved what no one else in her physical situation had achieved before.

Like Keller and Habakkuk, we are called to have vision. The Lord challenged Habakkuk to see what no one else could see and to make a note of it. Covey points out that habit number one toward success is to be a creator, but habit number two is the first creation. So, after we have accepted responsibility in productivity, we must write down the vision. We need to clearly articulate our vision if we are going to stay focused. Writing it down helps us to see on paper what we envision, and it also helps us to communicate to others who will help us. They can't help us if they don't understand what we are trying to achieve. We need a developed vision and not simply a random good idea. Rick Warren aptly sums it up:

> Writing down your purposes on paper will force you to think specifically about the path of your life. The Bible says, 'know where you are headed, and you will stay on solid ground' [Proverbs 4:26]. A life purpose statement not only spells out what you intend to do with your time, life, and money, but also implies what you aren't going to do. Proverbs says, 'An intelligent person aims at wise action, but a fool starts off in many directions' [Proverbs 17:24-26].[10]

Find Your Passion

Many times, we have great ideas. We get frustrated because nobody else has initiated what we think is best. Can't they see that this or that needs to be done? Why isn't anybody addressing this or that obvious issue? Sometimes, what we see frustrates us, and other times, what we see being neglected makes us angry. That's how passion works! The secret is that, when our mind's eye glimpses a vision, it is usually because we are the ones that are supposed to take initiative and do something. Again, Ruth Haley Barton offers keen insight. Concerning the issue of vision, she says,

We 'see' with new eyes that God's call on our life is so tightly woven into the fabric of our being [passion], so core to who we are, that to ignore it or to refuse it would be to jeopardize our well-being. If we were to try to compromise or to live it only halfway, we'd run the risk of plunging into emptiness and meaninglessness.[11]

History reveals that inventions are born out of passion to address what the inventors saw as problems, problems that they just could not ignore. The problems did not worry others the way that they worried the inventors. The problems kept them up at night and got them up early in the morning until the problems were solved. New discoveries emerged; new inventions were born.

For example, in the late-1800s and early-1900s, the need for an automatic oil cup for trains bothered Elijah McCoy. The son of former slaves so uniquely invented the oil-dripping cup that other attempts to make knock-offs could not compare. None of them worked like Elijah's did. When seeking to purchase automatic oil cups for their trains, knowledgeable engineers would ask for "the real McCoy."[12] Today, we still use the expression, "the real McCoy," when we want something that is authentic. The fact is African American Elijah McCoy had competitors, but they could not be "the real McCoy." Equally, no one can be the real you and me. We were born for our unique contributions.

Another example would be Madam C. J. Walker. In the late-1800s and early-1900s, Madam Walker developed a passion for African American women's beauty and hygiene.[13] She started out poor but worked hard, and when she died, she was one of the wealthiest women in the United States.

Madam C. J. Walker had many disadvantages. She was not afforded the opportunity for formal education, struggling during the reconstruction. She had no family inheritance or resource support system. But, she tapped into that inner passion to help her people, particularly women. With no "pattern" to follow, Madam C. J. Walker invented one product, "Madam Walker's Wonderful Hair Grower." From the success of this one hair care product, she catapulted the rest of her career, making beauty products and building cosmetology schools. Madam C. J. Walker did what had never been done in her community.

The key is to find your passion. Several years ago, a young lady said to me, "I don't have a purpose." I was deeply concerned that she felt that way, but I appreciated the fact that she would share with me how she felt. Over the years, I have observed that there are many people who feel that they don't have a purpose. When we understand the connection between purpose and passion, we will discover that we do have a passion. Many times, we overlook our purpose because we locate passion in a different compartment in our minds and pursue what each of our environments shape us into believing is worth pursuing as purpose.

So, during the conversation with the young lady, I first affirmed her feelings. Then, I tried my best to help her see that she does indeed have purpose. During the conversation, however, I discovered that she was comparing her gifts and talents with her friends' gifts and talents. We often do this even when we don't realize it. The young lady did not feel that she had matching gifts with her peers, so she resolved that she was deficient of purpose. Often, other people's apparent success or even current trends over-shadow our own sense of purpose. But, when we put our eyes on Christ and discover ourselves in Him, we notice our own God-given passions. God gave them to us for a purpose. They become our pathways to success. Bishop Jakes aptly speaks about this issue of connecting passion with purpose in his book, *Instinct.* He explains,

> If you can't stand to see bad hairdos, maybe you should consider becoming a stylist. If you loathe seeing dilapidated houses and peeling paint, then maybe you should consider being a contractor or interior designer. Does the plight of the homeless make you shudder? Your passion might lead you to work with a nonprofit to eradicate this pervasive problem. [14]

History reveals that trailblazers start with little material resources. People like McCoy, Walker, and countless others tapped into their passion. They worked hard with the little they had. History bears record that their passions made an indelible impression on society. With a similar insight into the value of passion, Bishop Jakes explains,

> Knowing what you love, as well as what you love to hate, can fuel your instincts in ways that provide a super octane boost to the engine of your success. [15]

It seems true. God uses our passions to bring us to our destiny, but we have to commit ourselves to the process of success.

Make It Work!

Getting something new going is always a challenge. The greatest temptation is to give up. We must develop the vision from beginning until the end. Covey calls this, "beginning with the end in mind." Beginning with the end in mind does not presuppose all of the twists and turns in life. However, it does suggest that we should have a grasp on where we will start and where we want to end up. In this way, we become leaders in success. The Lord calls us to be proactive and to lead in our own journey of success. We can't wait for somebody else to lead our vision, and we can't wait for somebody else to make our vision a reality. God has given us what it takes to succeed!

A poem that my high school teacher, Mrs. Ruth Purnell, required her students to learn—"Equipment," by Edgar A. Guest—continues to encourage me in my own journey:

> Figure it out for yourself, my lad,
> You've all that the greatest of men have had,
> Two arms, two hands, two legs, two eyes
> And a brain to use if you would be wise.
> With this equipment they all began,
> So start for the top and say, 'I can.'
>
> Look them over, the wise and great
> They take their food from a common plate,
> And similar knives and forks they use,
> With similar laces they tie their shoes.
> The world considers them brave and smart,
> But you've all they had when they made their
> start

You can triumph and come to skill,
You can be great if you only will.
You're well equipped for what fight you choose,
You have legs and arms and a brain to use,
And the man who has risen great deeds to do
Began his life with no more than you.

You are the handicap you must face,
You are the one who must choose your place,
You must say where you want to go,
How much you will study the truth to know.
God has equipped you for life, but He
Lets you decide what you want to be.

Courage must come from the soul within,
The man must furnish the will to win.
So figure it out for yourself, my lad.
You were born with all that the great have had,
With your equipment they all began,
Get hold of yourself and say: 'I can.'

Late-19th-Century and early-20th-Century African American Scientist and Professor at Tuskegee Institute, George Washington Carver, gleaned inspiration from Guest's "Equipment." It was his favorite poem. Carver intensely examined soybeans, peanuts, pecans, and sweet potatoes. With his creative genius, Carver discovered three hundred ways to use peanuts and many more ways to use soybeans, pecans, and sweet potatoes. We continue to use many of Carver's products today. His products include but are not limited to the following: salted peanuts, peanut butter, pancake flour, peanut flour, malted peanuts, meat substitutes, chocolate coated peanuts, chili sauce, peanut brittle, dry coffee, cream candy, instant coffee, chop suey sauce, mock oysters, mayonnaise, peanut meat loaf, shredded peanuts, peanut sprouts, peanut bisque powder, peanut tofu sauce, cooking oil, cream for milk, butter milk, mock meat, mock goose, mock duck, mock chicken, cheese cream, bar candy, peanut wafers, peanut hull stock food, molasses feed, laundry soap, sweeping compound, beverage for ice cream, peanut beverage flakes, blackberry punch, plum punch, evaporated peanut beverage, cherry punch, pineapple punch, rubbing oil, iron tonic, tannic acid, medicine similar to castor oil, emulsion for bronchitis, castor substitute, goiter treatment, laxatives, hand lotion, face lotion, face cream, vanishing cream, face bleach and tan remover, baby massage cream, shampoo, oil for hair and scalp, shaving cream, antiseptic soap, pomade for skin, peanut oil shampoo, printer ink, writing ink, rubber, washing powder, cleanser for hands, linoleum, soil conditioner, soap stock, and shoe and leather blacking. It is amazing how much we can imagine, discover, and produce when we focus. Carver got up every day and set his focus on crops, and the world is better from it!

Later, I will discuss the important role that community plays in destiny. Though, we must understand that no one else can define you and me better than we can define ourselves. The world is waiting on us to disclose our full potential. We can't all be famous, but we can all be successful in living faithfully and responsibly, according to the vision that God gives us. When we do, we summon support and help in ways that we could never have imagined.

We need to keep that important question on our minds: "Where am I going?" Let's not just answer, "Somewhere."

Name the "somewhere." Then, let the vision be your focus. The world may not understand it, but as with George Washington Carver, in years to come, our beneficiaries will be able to look back and see how much better their world became because we were here.

Keep It Moving!

Sometimes the very people who will benefit the most from our vision are the ones who can't see what we see. Often, they discourage us from stepping out there. They may even become skeptics rather than supporters. When skeptics are people who we depend on for moral support or resources, their cynicism often discourages us. I have learned that visionaries must find within themselves the will to keep it moving in the face of naysayers and doubters.

The old adage says, "Nothing beats a failure but a try." What makes the United States such a great nation (among other things) is the fundamental courage to try again and again. Keep going even when it does not work out quite the way that you thought. Learn from mistakes and keep it moving! Often, when God is doing something in and through us, others might not get it, but we must not stop. We must keep moving forward in the vision. In time, they will see.

Then, there are those who may not materially benefit from our vision because the outcome of the vision's fulfillment is not materialistic. The benefit of a vision may be a didactical, inspirational, or spiritual blessing. Yet, perhaps, the vision has a dynamic benefit with elements of all of the above. However, sometimes, benefits are not immediately discernible, particularly in the eyes of those who do not see what we see and know what we know. After all, the vision is our vision and not other people's vision—even when others are to become beneficiaries of our vision.

While Jesus was on the cross, He was moved with compassion for the people who did not understand God's vision for humanity's redemption, including the ones who were consenting to His gruesome death on the cross. Though He knew they just didn't get it, Jesus prayed, "Father, forgive them for they do not know what they are doing" (paraphrase of Luke 23:34a). Jesus saw beyond the moment and knew the benefit for them. They didn't. So, Jesus' response to his interlocutors was simply to forgive them and keep it moving! Soon, the world's eyes were open to see. He was more than just a man. He was a God-man on a mission!

Earlier, I mentioned that there have been times when I have lost sight of the forest for the trees. The minutia of particularities can overshadow our focus. Vision gets foggy. It seems easy to get distracted and lose course. This can happen when we become worried about what people think of us.

If you are like me, you care about people and what they think about you. This could be a gift in fields in which you have to deal with people, even difficult people—fields such as pastoral ministry, sociology, counseling, teaching, and others. The old saying, "People don't care how much you know until they know how much you care" (although true at some level) could become a stumbling block. We must care about the well-being of people but not so much about what they think of the vision that God gives to us. (Later, I will discuss the value and role of community.) However, we should not confuse the necessity of connections in community with the need for validation. It has been said, "We must know who we are, whose we are, and where we are going."

We will lose sight of destiny as soon as we start looking to others for vision. While we are attuned to people, their feelings, and their suggestions, we cannot lose sight of the higher calling, the goal, or the vision that God gives us. More than anything, we must pursue God's will for our lives. We must pursue it in a way that pleases God, a way that touches God's heart.

The Gospel story of the "Woman with the Issue of Blood" (Matt. 9:20-22; Mark 5:25-34; Luke 8:43-48) comes to mind. The nameless woman had an issue, but she was determined not to allow it to stop her from pursuing the solution. Beyond the problem itself, there were several factors that could have hindered her pursuit. There was a history of failed effort. She had exhausted her resources. It is highly probable that she had a reputation of having an incurable problem.

Now, according to Mark's account, there was a crowd between her and Jesus. Yet, this woman stayed focused on her vision to touch His garment. Undoubtedly, her issue of blood caused her to be a bit smelly, ostracized, and considered unwelcome by the crowd. The lesson for us here is that we cannot allow anything to deter us from the goal. Stated another way, don't let distractions destroy your vision.

Think about it. Here is a nameless woman with a long-standing issue of uncontrollable blood flow. The odds were against her. Going public to do something that had never been done was a rather risky thing to do. What if it doesn't work? This woman's beauty is revealed in her audacity to stay focused on what "she said to herself." She denied denial, resisted resistance, and kept her eyes on Jesus. Jesus was moved by her touch and healed her.

This woman teaches us that, despite the crowd, we have to aim with intensity and keep it moving. Her mind was on what she envisioned for herself: "If I only touch his [Jesus'] garment, I will be made well" (Matt. 9:21). What vision do you have for yourself? Are you letting what the crowd says or what you think they may think to deter you away from that vision? Though the woman with the issue of blood was not known, she has become well-known. Her story has inspired millions around the world.

Let's stay focused, move from the past, and keep it moving! There is another side; the future is waiting on us.

1. Mother Teresa, A Gift for God: Prayers and Meditations (New York: Harper Collins, 1996), 67.

2. Mother Teresa, "Keynote Address of Mother Teresa: Tokyo, April 22, 1982, International Symposium on Reverence for Life, sponsored by the Family Life Association." No page numbers. Online source. http://www2.cc.oshima-k.ac.jp/~ito/teresa/teresa_tokyo2.htm (accessed April 5, 2014).

3. Morris, 59.

4. Ibid.

5. D. Arcelious Harris, Facebook Post, March 9, 2014.

6. Tara Alami and Noor Louzi, "End Poverty Now." No page numbers. Online source: http://end-poverty-now.weebly.com/quotes--sayings.html (Accessed February 27, 2014).

7. Myles Munroe, *Understanding Your Potential: Discovering the Hidden You* (Shippensburg, PA: Destiny Image Publishers, 1991), Preface.

8. Covey, 70.

9. Ibid., 71.

10. Rick Warren, *The Purpose Driven Life: What On Earth Am I Here for?* (Grand Rapids, MI: Zondervan, 2002), 21. On Proverbs 4:26, Warren quotes from the Contemporary English Version of the Bible. On Proverbs 17:24-26, He quotes from the Good News Translation.

11. Barton, *Strengthening the Soul of Your Leadership*, 74.

12. *Lemelson MIT*, "Elijah McCoy: Automatic Oil Cup." No page numbers. Online Source. http://web.mit.edu/invent/iow/mccoy.html (accessed April 1, 2014).

13. *Lemelson MIT*, "Madam C. J. Walker: Hair Care Products." No page numbers. Online Source. http://web.mit.edu/invent/iow/cjwalker.html (Accessed April 1, 2014).

14. T. D. Jakes, *Instinct: The Power to Unleash Your Inborn Drives* (New York: Faith Words, 2014), 187.

15. Ibid.

3

EDUCATION:
THE PASSPORT TO SUCCESS

Education is our passport to the future, for tomorrow belongs to the people who prepare for it today.

—Malcolm X

SOLOMON WAS YOUNG when his dad, David, died. He was to be the next king of Israel. How would he do it? He had many people to lead, a nation to fortify, a building to build for God, enemies to deal with, decisions to make, and a God to please. This was a lot for a young man to deal with. He has no experience in these areas, but he wanted to succeed.

So, with the insuperable feat ahead of him, Solomon and the children of Israel went to the tabernacle of the Lord to pray. According to 2 Chronicles 1:7, during worship, God invited Solomon, "Ask what I [God] shall give you." The young king's response was brilliant. Solomon prayed this prayer:

> You have shown great and steadfast love to David my father, and have made me king in his

place. O Lord God, let your word to David my father be now fulfilled, for you have made me king over a people as numerous as the dust of the earth. Give me now *wisdom* and *knowledge* to go out and come in before this people, for who can govern this people of yours, which is so great?" (2 Chr. 1:8–10)

The young king did not ask for material possessions or for vindication concerning his enemies. Instead, he asked for *chokmah*, which is Hebrew for "wisdom" (the root is *chakam*, which means "to become wise in mind, word, and action")[1] and *madda*, which is Hebrew for "knowledge" (the root is *yada*, which means "to gain instructions").[2]

The Hebrew term, *chokmah*, means "cleverness of skills and prudence in both religious affairs and in leadership." The Hebrew term, *madda*, means "developed intelligence, a sharp mind, endowed with information." In other words, Solomon is asking God for education! Solomon's request impresses God. Of all that Solomon could ask for, he chooses *chokmah* and *madda*. As stated in Scripture,

God answered Solomon, 'Because this was in your heart, and you have not asked for possessions, wealth, honor, or the life of those who hate you, and have not even asked for long life, but have asked for wisdom and knowledge for yourself that you may govern my people over whom I have made you king, wisdom and knowledge are granted to you. I will also give you riches, possessions, and honor, such as none of the kings had who were before you, and none after you shall have the like.' (2 Chr. 1:11–12)

There are at least two important lessons from Solomon's story that explain how education is a godly principle for success. The first lesson is that Solomon showed a remarkable measure of maturity. As a young, new king, he understood that wisdom and knowledge are consequential to a successful kingdom.

Second, we learn something about God. God is the fundamental source of all wisdom and true knowledge. Solomon trusted that dependence on God for wisdom and knowledge would maximize his leadership.

Dr. Benjamin Carson, Sr. was the 2014 Commencement Speaker at Regent University. In his speech, he eloquently asserted a memorable comment on the value of knowledge: "Knowledge is a formidable foe for falsehood and a formidable ally of truth." Solomon succeeded as king, and he left a legacy of having been the wisest man who ever lived because early in his career he placed premium emphasis on divine truth. Solomon was a successful leader as a consequence of his hunger for God's truth through his search for His wisdom and knowledge.

Consider this. If God gives us material gain without wisdom and knowledge, we will enjoy it for only a little while. But, if God grants us wisdom and knowledge, significant gain will follow, and it will be sustainable as well. This reminds me of the old saying, "If you give a man a fish, he will eat for a day. But, if you show the man how to fish, he will eat many days." The lessons are similar. Education is an important key in long-term success. As Christians, it is wise that we grasp hold of the essentiality of education. As with

Solomon, it pleases God when we seek wisdom and knowledge as principles for success.

Get Learning with Your Burning

Education (wisdom and knowledge) is powerful! Yet, many people do not seem to understand the value of education. I place education within the category of Christian virtues. As stated earlier, Plato considered virtues to be vital skills and dispositions that everyone needs in order to reach holistic human well-being. Scripture presents a God who wants for us to reach the fullness of our potential in Christ.

Poor educational resources stifle the fullness of human potential. Hosea recorded the Lord saying, "My people are destroyed for lack of knowledge; because you have rejected knowledge, I reject you" (Hosea 4:6). Herein lies the foundation for education as a godly virtue. Without it, we live on the precipice of an abyss. Lord, show us the pathway to holistic education!

It is surprising that many Spirit-filled Christians continue to struggle to reconcile the Holy Spirit and education. I have spoken with many Christians who feel that their faith leads and guides them intuitively. So, there is little value placed on the search for knowledge in a formal way. Historically, this has been particularly true in some Protestant Christian traditions. In some Pentecostal-Charismatic perspectives, a critical mind is considered to be the devil's playground as it is seen as competing with the Spirit. There has been a bit of unsettled contention concerning whether or not formal education is a viable mechanism for the Spirit as a means for preparing the mind for God's work in the world.

I am a son of the Pentecostal tradition. Thankfully, our family emphasized the value of education toward holistic development in the Christian's success. We believed in the need for "learning" (formal educational pursuits) as a useful tool to accompany the "burning" (the baptism of the Spirit).

The Spirit Teaches

Christians, including Pentecostals, have always believed that the Spirit teaches because the Bible says so. For instance, John 14:26 states, "But the Helper, the Holy Spirit, whom the Father will send in my name, he will *teach* you all things." Yet, some Evangelicals and Pentecostals struggle to understand the parameters concerning the ways in which the Spirit teaches. According to 1 John 22:27,

> ...the anointing that you received from him abides in you, and you have no need that anyone should teach you. But as his anointing *teaches* you about everything, and is true, and is no lie—just as it has taught you, abide in him.

A Spirit-filled mind enlarges our capacity to absorb what we need to know for success. Moreover, I have learned that there are multiple avenues through which the Spirit is able to teach however the Spirit chooses. As they say, "the proof is in the pudding!"

It seems highly likely that a God of order and structure is able to use organized systems of learning to help to facilitate the discovery of truth and light. Theologian Amos Yong points out that a Spirit-led search of knowledge cultivates and nurtures a distinctive way of lifelong learning that is indeed consistent with the Spirit-filled life to which Christians are called.[3] Christian education, broadly understood, becomes a way of growing in the Lord while also developing in those God-given skills and talents that will put food on the table and a roof over our heads. In other words, education as a virtue is both spiritual and material. As stated in previous chapters, true success includes all of the above.

To grasp this concept, we must ask ourselves, "How do I understand the relationship between God and education, the Holy Spirit and education, and Jesus and education? Stated another way, I often ask my students a question that my dissertation chairman, Dale P. Andrews (from Boston University School of Theology), asked me: "What is your theology of education?" When Andrews asked me this question, I did not know how to answer it at first. What a thought-provoking question! I had not thought of it in that way before he asked. Every Christian should seriously question the issue of education in reference to God.

I am convinced that God cares that we study to learn as much as we can. In fact, the Spirit teaches. In 1 John 2:27, the evangelist cautions that the Spirit teaches, emphasizing that learning is divinely-initiated and facilitated rather than human-initiated and facilitated. Human beings are merely vessels for divine facilitation. Additionally, the evangelist warns against human intervention in the Spirit-oriented learning process.

We absolutely need divine intervention in human ambition. We must open up our minds and hearts to hear and identify where God is within the educational process. Because God is a God of knowledge, we must understand that education is an important Christian virtue.

In 1 Thessalonians 4:13, Romans 1:3, and 1 Corinthians 10:1, Paul advances a theology of education. He says, "I do not want you to be unaware." Education is about awareness. I have met so many people who worked hard throughout their young lives. At 55 years old, they want to retire but can't. How would they pay for stuff? They have worked for 30 years or more and never invested toward retirement. When asked why they didn't invest all of those years in Roth IRAs, mutual funds, life insurances, stocks, etc., their common response is, "I didn't know about all that." The highway to a dead-end is "I didn't know about all that."

As a Spirit-filled Christian, I have learned that a key role of the Holy Spirit is that of divine agency for learning. John 14:26 says, "The Holy Spirit teaches all things…" Theologically speaking, this means that God cares about the life of the mind, the issue of learning. God created us with the capacity to learn. Part of God's self in the Holy Spirit facilitates learning in complex ways. The Holy Spirit uses revelation knowledge, and the Spirit facilitates learning through books, schools, etc. In other words, constructive education pleases God. As a liberating God, He is a God of knowledge. Knowledge unlocks the prisons and frees us to pursue boundless success!

Moreover, Jesus viewed the liberating power of the Spirit as so important that, in Luke 4:18, He began his ministry with an inaugural reading from Isaiah 61:1–2a:

> The Spirit of the Lord God is upon me, because the Lord has anointed me to bring good news to the poor; he has sent me to bind up the broken-hearted, to proclaim liberty to the captives, and

the opening of the prison to those who are bound;
to proclaim the year of the Lord's favor.

This passage is central to my own theology as it seemed central to that of Jesus. There is a lot here. The significance of this passage to the role of the Spirit in education, however, lies in the relationship between the Spirit and the liberation of the captives, the prison emancipation for those who are bound. The language of incarceration rings like the physical county jail, state prisons, or federal penitentiaries. Spiritually, we often think of prisons as some negative habit, addiction, or sinful way of thinking or living. Few people think of prisons as mental captivities to quarantine us from our potential success, but why not think in these terms? Certainly, if the Spirit is able to liberate us from physical and spiritual prisons, the Spirit is also able to emancipate us from the prisons of our minds.

Paul teaches that Christ gives us

> ...divine power to destroy strongholds. We destroy arguments and every lofty opinion that rises against the knowledge of God, and take every thought captive to obey Christ.
> (2 Cor. 10:4b–5)

Paul's teaching is applicable here. If God gives us vision for success, we have power in the Spirit to destroy any stronghold of arguments and opinions that oppose what God has given to us. How do we destroy arguments and opinions? Education becomes the Spirit's tool to liberate the mind toward any God-kind of successful achievement.

A Mind is a Terrible Thing to Waste

Growing up, annually, my siblings and I would gather around the television to watch the "Lou Rawls Parade of Stars," a show to raise money for the United Negro College Fund (UNCF). Lou became famous for branding the UNCF's tag line since 1972: "A mind is a terrible thing to waste." In 1944, emerging through Jim Crow Era, the founders of the UNCF, Frederick D. Patterson (president of Tuskegee Institute), Mary McLeod Bethune (founder of Bethune-Cookman College), and others were convinced that the mind possessed the capacity to transform people and, eventually, society.

My brothers and I met Lou Rawls in the late-1990s. Our group, A7, and Lou Rawls appeared the same night on the Candi Staton Show at the TBN studios in Atlanta, Georgia. Lou was a funny guy as well as a very talented singer and actor. We had a lot of fun that night. He was, also, very complementary of my brothers' and my formal educational aspirations. Lou said something that has stuck with me as I had also heard others say something similar. He said, "Well, I graduated from the 'School of Hard Knocks'." Then, he led us in a burst of laughter. He didn't go into details about what he meant, but he was probably referring to the summation of life events that taught him important lessons over the years. Or, perhaps, he was referring to his car crash in 1958. He was pronounced dead until the doctors determined that he was actually severely injured and was in a coma for several days. Usually, the "School of Hard Knocks" refers to the summation of the ups-and-downs of life's experiences from which one learns without ever enrolling into formal training.

I have learned over the years that experience is a significant teacher, but it is not the best teacher. It is much better to learn from others' experiences. In doing so, we are able to avoid unnecessary headaches and heartaches that come with the "School of Hard Knocks". This type of education comes in several forms. For example, it could be adherence to informal advice from those who have gone down a road that we are thinking about going. It could be submitting to regular training. It could be enrolling in certification programs or getting a college education. All forms of constructive learning have potential for broadening our imaginations, emancipating our minds from the prison of ignorance and catapulting us toward success.

African-American history teaches us that our forefathers and foremothers fought for more humane treatment and Civil Rights. People like Bishop Richard Allen and, later, Booker T. Washington and then Mary McLeod Bethune believed in the power of lifting the veil of ignorance from the African's face. That power is defined not only by the abolition of slavery and by gaining Civil Rights but also by the freedom that comes through education.

As an African American, I have always felt connected to the "freedom through education" legacy that suffering African-American slaves and (later) African-American matriarchs and patriarchs of the Jim Crow Era handed down to us. They understood that the "School of Hard Knocks" tends to render knocks that are harder than necessary. They wanted their children and grandchildren to live a better life than the ones they had. They recognized that their generation's limited access to knowledge also limited their opportunities. So, they organized training centers, schools, and colleges as an investment in their children's futures.

Churches participated in the vision for schools because they determined that formal education could be a viable mechanism for the Spirit to prepare God's young people for boundless success.

Formal education is one way to learn from the experiences, experiments, and explorations that others have had. Their learned lessons serve as important lessons to liberate us from ignorance so that we can have futures of promise. For example, New York Theological Seminary has a North Campus located behind the Max-A prison walls of Sing Sing Prison in Ossining, New York. They offer a master's degree in public service. Over the past 25 or more years of the program, studies have shown that formal education proves powerful in lowering the high percentage of recidivism rates. New York Theological Seminary reports,

> The unique, fully accredited MPS program has a recidivism rate of under ten percent. It continues to turn around the lives of not only the sixteen or so students each year, but also the prisoners they serve while incarcerated and the people they serve once they are released.[4]

True emancipation is that of the mind. History teaches us that societies that emphasize education produce the sharp minds that impact common good. As referenced in the previous chapter, Edgar A. Guest's "Equipment" teaches us that we have the same equipment that everyone else before us had. The main equipment that we have is our minds. We waste our minds when we don't invest time in study and productive discussion. With so many potential distractions—various opportunities, vices, people, and other things—we must put forth extra effort to stay focused on using our minds constructively. The most constructive way to use our minds is to read, study, and learn.

Is it Positive? Then, Read It!

During my days at Candler School of Theology at Emory University, I met with my Old Testament professor, the late Dr. John Hays, in his office to get some professional advice. I was particularly interested in becoming a theological educator. So, as I explained my interested to Dr. Hays that day, he listened carefully and was very supportive of my educational aspirations. With a mouth-full of tobacco, Dr. Hays leaned back in his chair and took a spit. He cut his eyes up toward me and responded in his Southern twang, "Antipas, if you want to be a scholar, read everything that you can get your hands on. If you see a piece of paper on the floor, read it. Get some books, read them." I thought, "Hmm, so that is how he became so smart!" I stored his words in my heart. That day, I learned that scholarship is not a degree; scholarship is education. Education means to be in search for answers to questions.

Inquisitive minds look for information. They ask questions. I have always been a rather curious person. But, like many people who are hungry for knowledge, the people around us don't always understand that hunger. They often label us as "nosey" or say that we ask "too many questions." The scorn of pejorative labels is off-putting. I began to think that I was wrong for having so many questions. Over the years, I have learned that there are no silly, stupid, or inappropriate questions. Even when there are no clear answers, without the questions, we will never know the answers. In fact, sometimes, it is healthy to continue asking the questions. Questions lead to new discoveries and new inventions even when a new discovery does not respond neatly to the original inquiry.

Dr. Hays helped me to discover that an inquisitive mind is a gift to fresh discovery, even in scholarship. A deep-seated desire to learn reveals the potential for knowledge. Properly channeled, an inquisitive mind drives the work of many of the world's greatest contributors in many fields, from the science laboratory to the ball field.

You may have read it before. It is true. No one can know enough, especially leaders. Our minds should always be on a mission to learn. As they say, "learn all you can and can all you learn." The point here is that we should store as much knowledge as possible. In time, we will need it. While we should study with particular interest in the direction of our goals, there is a thing called, "knowledge transfer." Knowledge transference speaks to the mind's ability to convert learning in one area for application in a somewhat unrelated area.

The mind is a genius piece of equipment that God has given to maximize our potential. As long as this equipment is functioning sufficiently, we have the same opportunity for success as anyone.

It Pays to Know Something

For many years, the motto of the Accelerated Christian Education (ACE) curriculum has been that "Christian education doesn't cost; it pays." This philosophy contends that there is an intrinsic necessity of faith both in the life of the spirit and in the life of the mind. Education, both formal education and general knowledge, pays the debt of igno-rance and can even save lives.

To rising sixth graders at the Urban Youth Summer Academy at Regent University, the former president of Regent University, Carlos Campo, used Danny Boyle's *127 Hours*[5] as an illustration to explain the power of knowledge. The movie is based on a true story. Climber Aron Ralston found himself trapped alone in a narrow Utah canyon. His arm was stuck between a boulder and a wall. Aron could not escape his arm from the trap. For days, he was there. Then, the blood was no longer circulating in the arm–it was dead. Soon, he would die! What would he do?

Dr. Campo argued that knowledge saved Ralston's life. He determined that the best way to save his own life was to perform Do-It-Yourself (DIY) surgery. He used the rock to snap his own arm off and thereby saved his life. While it took astonishing courage to make this decision, I am baffled with the thought, "What if Ralston didn't know that per-forming DIY surgery was a workable option?" He would have died alone in a cave without considering this option. Indeed, it pays to be in the know!

Education is a biblical concept. As stated earlier, Hosea states, "My people are destroyed for lack of knowledge; be-cause you have rejected knowledge, I reject you" (Hosea 4:6). Also, Isaiah says, "Therefore my people go into exile for lack of knowledge; their honored men go hungry, and their multitude is parched with thirst" (Isaiah 5:13). In other words, without knowledge, people are impoverished of nat-ural and spiritual sustenance.

Education Is the Most Powerful Weapon

On July 16, 2003, South African President (and now, the late) Nelson Mandela launched his Mindset Network. At the Planetarium of the University of the Witwatersrand in Johannesburg, South Africa, the title of his talk was, "Lighting Your Way to a Better Future." Mandela boldly expressed, "Education is the most powerful weapon which you can cause to change the world."[6] This was particularly powerful for him to say against the backdrop of heinous apartheid and black South African violent retaliation against that hostile regime. But, Mandela proved correct. As a young man hungry for education and service for his people, Mandela was not satisfied with his own advantage to study at the university. He, moreover, wanted to lift the veil of oppression on behalf of his people in South Africa during the heinous apartheid system. During the rise of black South African retaliation against white South African brutality, Mandela led the African National Congress to return to their original peaceful protest that resulted in the ending of apartheid. After 27 years of incarceration and many more years of Dutch oppression inflicted upon black South Africans, education and courage were essential in Mandela's preparation to crush the ignorance of South African apartheid. Today, Black South Africa is advancing through the power of education.

One would observe that many impoverished countries suffer from low quality education. Also, any nation that is destitute of spiritual depth and ethical pursuit suffers spiritually. With Hosea 4:6 in mind, I would argue that a spiritual hunger is not only theological but also educational. The United States of America experienced the height of its preeminence as a nation when this country placed a unified emphasis on Christian values and made room for spirituality in the public square. Notably, we were, then, leaders in quality education.

Where the Rubber Hits the Road

Indeed, knowledge is powerful, yet it is the application of cognitive deposits that makes the difference. What good is it to know something but fail to use that knowledge? If I know how to cook a meal and there are adequate ingredients to prepare it, what good is it to know how to cook without cooking? I need to put that knowledge to work by producing the meal! The same is true in any area of life. We need to learn, but we need to produce something worthwhile with that learning.

Even in business, to know something without exercising that information for the benefit of the company is simply foolish. With more than 25 years in business, Leanne Haogland-Smith comments in her blog, "Exceptional business professionals are those who apply knowledge."[7] Application is the process by which we convert what is in our heads into action. Action expresses observable value to what we know. As pertaining to education, action is where the rubber hits the road.

Application of knowledge is fueled by intuition. To borrow language from Bishop T. D. Jakes, it is called, "instinct." Intuition or instinct can be understood as "wisdom." In other words, going to school and attaining information is not the sum total of what it takes.

In the situation of Solomon, he asked God for education, but he had an instinct that prompted him to seek education.

Then, he needed that same instinct to apply the knowledge and wisdom. As Bishop Jakes says, "Degrees do not deliver success on their own."[8] We must bring education full circle with academics and instincts. They are not contrary to each other. Strong academic inquiry is pursued out of intellectual curiosity and instinctive impulses. The Holy Spirit fuels the process, resulting in a solid education.

A Caveat: The Danger of Echo-ology

Success demands that we listen and learn information that we might not agree with or that may even be heretical. We must not simply listen to information that echoes what we already know or opinions that we already have. I call that echo-ology. Studying information or ideas that we already think and believe reinforces those ideas but does little to feed the hunger to know more.

If all truth is God's truth, we can discover God's truth wherever God chooses to expose it. God is bigger than what we already know. So, to learn more of God's truth, we must be open to His multiple ways of teaching and guiding for our lives.

Discernment of spirits is crucial in discovering and deciphering valuable information for the journey ahead. As the saying goes, "eat the meat and throw out the bones." But, don't miss out on valuable information because you don't want to hear something that you might not agree with. When the principle of education is appropriated fully, we might discover the next mystery of life, the answer to world peace, the cure for diseases, the flying car, or the next innovative technological solution.

1. F. Brown, S. Driver, and C. Briggs, *The Brown, Driver, Briggs Hebrew and English Lexicon* (Hendrickson, MA: 2000), 314.

2. Ibid., 393.

3. Amos Yong, "Finding the Holy Spirit at a Christian University: Renewal and the Future of Higher Education in the Pentecostal/Charismatic Tradition. In *Spirit-Empowered Christianity in the 21st Century*, edited by Vinson Synan (Lake Mary, FL: Charisma House, 2011), 476.

4. New York Theological Seminary, "NTS' Sing Sing Program." No page numbers. Online source: http://www.nyts.edu/sing-sing-program/ (Accessed July 8, 2014).

5. See Patrick Barkham, "The extraordinary story behind Danny Boyle's 127 Hours" in *The Guardian*, Tuesday, December 14, 2010. No page numbers. Online source: http://www.theguardian.com/film/2010/dec/15/story-danny-boyles-127-hours (Accessed February 12, 2014).

6. Nelson Mandela, "Lighting your way to a better future." On website for the Nelson Mandela Foundation. No page numbers. Online source http://db.nelsonmandela.org/speeches/pub_view.asp?pg=item&ItemID=NMS909 (accessed April 3, 2014).

7. Leanne Haogland-Smith, "Knowledge is Power – But, Applying Knowledge is More Powerful!" Online: No page numbers: https://www.salesgravy.com/sales-articles/advice-for-sales-professionals/knowledge-is-power-but-applying-knowledge-is-more-powerful.html (accessed January 2, 2014).

8. T. D. Jakes, Lecture at Regent University, "The Leadership Institute with T. D. Jakes Based on the Book *Instinct: The Power to Unleash Your Inborn Drive*." Thursday, March 20th, 2014 @ Founders Inn, Thursday, March 20, 2014.

4

HUMBLENESS IS THE WAY

Before honor is humility.

—Proverbs 18:12

GROWING UP, I LEARNED that "Humbleness is the Way." Careful study reveals that the formally educated and uneducated people, the religious and the pagan people, philosophers and theologians, the wealthy and the poor agree that humility is an indispensable virtue for authentic success.

Pastor and theologian Richard Gula points out that to properly understand humbleness or humility is to locate the word "humility" in light of its Latin root, *humus (earth)*, a word that is also the origin of the word, "human."[1] Gula further notes that humility means to be down to earth about one's self.

In Scripture, Paul teaches the churches in Rome to be down to earth in the way that they think about themselves. He says, "I say to everyone among you not to think of himself [and herself] more highly than he [and she] ought to think" (Romans 12:3a). Being down to earth does not mean to deny our gifts but rather to be honest about our limitations. Gula explains that humility like this is possible when we have acquired the appropriate amount of self-esteem without arrogance.[2] Humility demands a certain amount of self-esteem. Without self-esteem, humility is threatened by the lack of confidence. We need confidence to achieve as well as to be humble. In this way, self-esteem and confidence belong on the side of humility—not contrary to it.

People who are confident recognize that their personal gifts have limitations. When we are comfortable with who we are, it is much easier to listen and learn from others.

M. De Voltaire recounts several philosophical teachings on humility's indispensability to self-esteem and the harmful impact of arrogance in Plato, Epictetus, Marcus Antoninus, Descartes, Rousseau, and Father Viret. Voltaire concludes that the proper way to think of humility has to do with "the modesty of the soul."[3] Soulish modesty is confident but not boastful. It plays itself out beyond the soul in the way that we deal with people and situations. It propels us forward in success; humility never suppresses success.

Humility requires self-esteem without arrogance. In this chapter, I wish to explain how a humble approach to life and work embraces self-esteem but avoids arrogance at all costs.

Listen and Learn

Self-esteem and arrogance are contradicting concepts. Self-esteem means to understand who we are with the confidence to acknowledge the need for others to help us in areas of our weaknesses. Arrogance means to imagine our gifts as being greater than the need to listen to others. Arrogant people don't know who they are. They tend to spend a lot of time trying to prove that they know more than they do, that they are more important than someone else, and that they are more successful than they are.

Speaking more personally, other attributes that we are likely to exemplify when we are not humble are the following: We want to teach more than we listen. We want to lead more than we want to be led. We want accolades for our contributions more than we want to compliment others. We want to talk about ourselves more than we want to learn about others.

Listening is more important than talking. There is an old saying that is worthy of our adaptation: "It pays to listen!" I believe that the margin of success that I have experienced has a lot to do with listening. I only wish that I had listened more. I certainly endeavor to listen more today. Proverbs 1:5 states, "Let the wise hear and increase in learning, and the one who understands obtain guidance." Success is born out of the willingness to listen and learn and to observe and absorb.

Relax and Let God Lift You Up

In the Gospel of Luke, Jesus tells a parable to explain the practical benefits of humility, a valuable lesson for those of us in pursuit of the God-kind of success. Luke 18:9-14 states,

> He also told this parable to some who trusted in themselves that they were righteous, and treated others with contempt: "Two men went up into the temple to pray, one a Pharisee and the other a tax collector. The Pharisee, standing by himself, prayed thus: 'God, I thank you that I am not like

other men, extortioners, unjust, adulterers, or even like this tax collector. I fast twice a week; I give tithes of all that I get.' But the tax collector, standing far off, would not even lift up his eyes to heaven, but beat his breast, saying, 'God, be merciful to me, a sinner!' I tell you, this man went down to his house justified, rather than the other. For everyone who exalts himself will be humbled, but the one who humbles himself will be exalted.

How ironic! A spiritual principle for everyday success sounds something like this. We have to get down in order to go up. It reminds me of when Micah and I were at a Sandals Resort in Montego Bay, Jamaica, for our third anniversary. I decided to learn to swim. Micah was going to help me learn to float, but I was having the hardest time floating. You know why? I was trying too hard. I was not relaxing. Instinctively, I was fighting the water. Micah said to me, "Antipas, don't be afraid of drowning. Just lay back, relax, and don't allow yourself to feel like you are drowning. Then, you will float." I did it. And you know what happened? Yes. I floated out into the middle of the clear blue waters. The lesson here is that, when we let go of trying too hard to shine and just relax in God, we will see God's hand of success in our lives.

Don't be a Know-it-All

One challenging task is to maintain humility in areas where we feel that we are most talented or qualified. Let me explain it this way. My brother, Norman Andronicus (we call him, "Duke"), is an attorney in Florida. He has an undergraduate degree in English and excelled among his peers as a college student, having been appointed by the Chair of the English Department as the Student Director of the Writing Center at LaGrange College. He graduated with honors and was subsequently hired as an adjunct professor to teach grammar and composition for the LaGrange College evening class. He helped all seven of our siblings, our parents, and me with our writing projects, as well. As an English major, he was positioned for success in the legal field.

As a young practicing attorney with an academic background in English, Duke would assist other attorneys with legal research and writing, particularly, memorandums of law, briefs, and settlement proposals. When he was struggling as a solo practitioner, one of his mentors associated with Duke on a personal injury case. Duke's primary assignment was to do legal research and draft the pleadings and motions. In this case, the opposing counsel filed a motion for summary judgment. Duke's job was to do research and draft an objection to the defendant's motion for summary judgment and brief in support thereof. Duke submitted the final draft to his mentor, and his mentor gave him a raving review. The objection and brief were filed, and the defendant's motion was heard. As a result of Duke's research and writing, his mentor prevailed in court and the defendant's motion for summary judgment was denied.

Not long thereafter, Duke expressed an interest to merge his solo practice with an attorney who has distinguished himself as a well-respected expert in his profession as a criminal and personal injury attorney. When asked by this attorney for a legal writing sample, Duke eagerly submitted as his sample legal writing the previous objection to the defendant's motion for summary judgment and brief in support thereof that he had drafted for his mentor. To Duke's surprise, this attorney was highly critical of the brief that he was so proud of.

Duke called me and said, "Man, he ripped up my brief. But I am not going to get defensive. I want to learn."

I asked if the guy was an English major.

Duke replied, "No! He has an undergraduate degree in Accounting."

However, this attorney has been practicing law for a number of years longer than my brother. Duke realized that irrespective of his successes as a writer, he could benefit from the knowledge and experience of a seasoned attorney who has much more experience in inking and organizing legal theories and arguments. Only a few months later, Duke had a conversation with this established attorney, and this attorney complemented him for his analytical gifts and aggression as a young attorney. He invited Duke to join his successful law firm. Duke eagerly accepted the offer but had a moment of shock that the offer was extended because of the experience with the brief, but this was an example of what it means to humble one's self and then to be lifted up!

Similarly, my friend and mentor, the late German scholar Roswith Gerloff, ripped my dissertation into pieces. I had to suck it up and listen. In the end, I got the dissertation published with Emeth Academic Press! Also, at the risk of seeming boastful, I would mention that before she died, Gerloff told a close colleague and confidante on her deathbed, Antipas' work is important. She furthermore requested that I write a chapter in her *Festifshif* that will be published posthumously. I was deeply moved when I heard the report.

What if I had not listened to her helpful critique of my work? What if I acted defensively, trying to explain this or that? What if I had arrogantly dismissed her critical feedback on the work? I may not have successfully completed the dissertation. I may not have landed the publishing deal. I would not have had the privilege of participating in her important *Festifshif*. To borrow my parents' words, "It pays to listen; humbleness is the way!"

Don't be a Self-by-Self

We all have gifts. We work hard and develop into individuals of distinction. But, if we are not careful, we could become victims of distinction. Distinctions become problems when we allow our individuality to become offensive to community. Solomon's wisdom teaches us,

> Two are better than one, because they have a good reward for their toil. For if they fall, one will lift up his fellow. But woe to him who is alone when he falls and has not another to lift him up! (Eccl. 4:9-10)

It takes humility, moreover, for one to accept the rewards of community over her or his own self-perceived smarts. Community demands that we submit to others in ways that challenge our ideas and even, at times, suppress our gifts. But, to suppress our gifts does not mean the same as to oppress our gifts. To suppress gifts or ideas means the same as the horse trainer when she pulls on an eager horse to run his way. The purpose is to contain the energy and redirect it in a constructive manner. In like manner, the type of suppression of gifts that is healthy helps to give equilibrium to our gifts or ideas for effective execution when appropriate.

To oppress gifts or ideas is quite different. Oppression is a means of devaluing gifts and ideas, suggesting that they are of no use.

We have to learn what it means to work together, arranging our gifts and ideas in a constructive manner to ensure communal productivity. If we don't suppress them inappropriately for communal living, we veer into individualism. Individualistic lifestyles begin and end in self-centeredness.

This principle applies in several areas of communal living and working, and it also applies in marriage. Sometimes, I have to remind myself about this. I was 34 when I got married, and I had lived alone for many years. I had developed many traditions. Now, I am married, and my wife has something to offer. She knows some things that I don't know. She has some good ideas, too. If I am too steeped in individualistic arrogance, I will miss out on some important and healthy opportunities for mutual growth.

The night that Judas betrayed Jesus to be crucified was eye-opening in so many ways (see John 13:2–17). After dinner, Jesus took the towel and washed His disciples' feet. John 13:3 points out that Jesus bowed down on the floor to wash their feet, "knowing that the Father had given all things into his hands, and that he had come from God and was going back to God." In other words, Jesus was assured of whom He was and of what divine gifts he possessed. He knew all along that He was God. This truth did not just occur to Him after the resurrection. Yet, Jesus demonstrated a universal truth.

There is no divine exaltation except for through submitting our gifts at the feet of others to serve them, even at the feet of those who clearly do not have our best interest at heart. Yes, Jesus even washed Judas' feet, knowing that He was going to turn on Him.

When Jesus got up from washing each of His disciples' feet, He commissioned them to do as He had done. An important lesson here is that Jesus wants us to rise to our full potential. He wants us to succeed in all of our God-ordained endeavors. Yet, just as Jesus did, we must remain in the service of others. In fact, all of our success is about serving others. In the community of mutual bowing and self-emptying to serve, we elevate to everything that God has for us.

Somebody Else Has Gifts, Too

Have you ever worked with someone who is hard to work with? They think that because they know something about the job, they can forge forward without following direction from a supervisor. They don't see the need to listen to a co-worker. They think they need to teach everybody else. They act like their way is the only right way to accomplish a task and that their perspective is the only correct one. They are opinionated so much so that they belittle other perspectives by devaluing other people's opinions. Soon, people resent working with them. Before you know it, they are in isolation and may even get fired. In reference to these kinds of people, we say, "Somebody else knows something, too!"

The path to success is paved with collaborations of one sort or another. We must learn to work with others. Admittedly, that can be difficult at times. But, when we learn how to collaborate with others, we either learn new lessons or re-inforce lessons that we have already learned. Either way, learning to work with others is a good thing. Success is always the byproduct of a series of collaborations. There is no value in being a know-it-all. A know-it-all turns people off and aborts success. When the Lord blesses us with a job, even if it is not our dream job, it is prudent to take a collaborative approach to the job and be willing to try new ideas. Humility, in general, has to do with the attitude by which we approach a situation, our co-workers, and the job itself.

I don't mean to suggest that we should be timid. We don't have to pretend as if we don't know anything. That would create an adverse situation as well. Bruna Martinuzzi clarifies the difference between humility and timidity in this way:

> We often confuse humility with timidity. Humility is not clothing ourselves in an attitude of self-denigration. Humility is all about maintaining our pride about who we are, about our achievements, about our worth – but without arrogance – it is the antithesis of hubris, that excessive, arrogant pride which often leads to the derailment of some corporate heroes, as it does with the downfall of the tragic hero in Greek drama… Humility is also a meta-virtue. It crosses into an array of principles. For example, we can safely declare that there can't be authenticity without humility. Why? Because, there is always a time in a leader's journey when one will be in a situation of not having all the answers. Admitting this and seeking others' input requires some humility.[4]

A key value of humility includes a posture to learn without making a fool of one's self. Bruce Lee once said, "Showing off is the fool's idea of glory."[5] The problem with such glory is that it reveals strengths in a distasteful manner but also embarrassingly exposes weaknesses. We have no need to try to shine brighter than others. We can always learn from others. Gula points out that humility is the willingness to do what we can as part of the action but that we

> ...do not have to be the whole show. They can let go of what is beyond their ability and beyond their control and invite others to share the burden and the benefit.[6]

It is prudent, moreover, to position ourselves in a learning mode even when we are providing output. People notice genius even when they don't acknowledge their observation. In due time, it will come to light. Yet, the glory of acknowledgement is not what success is all about.

Do It for the Right Reasons

Furthermore, some people are task-oriented. They believe that doing this or that will earn them greatness. At times, those same people find it difficult to serve in ways that are not so self-serving. They find it difficult to help out at the homeless shelter, a soup kitchen, or the convalescence home. They find it difficult to change an adult sick relative's diaper, rake somebody's yard, and the like. We often want the paid employment offer, the promotion on the job with accelerated pay, the pat on the back, or the most prestigious awards. We strive for greatness in ways that trump the need to develop in humility. In essence, we often do what we do for the wrong reasons, thinking success is on the other side of it all.

However, I have learned that success is not the financial compensation at the end of the day. It is not the award posted on the wall or the article in the newspaper. Success is best defined in the way that Martin Luther King, Jr. defines greatness in his 1968 sermon, "Drum Major Instinct," which he gleaned from Mark 10:35ff. He explained that everybody wants to be praised because of a real drum major instinct that rests within each person from birth. It even causes us to live above our means. We want to be great. We want to appear greater than we are. So, we try to live, ride, and look great. However, in his sermon on February 4th, 1968, King explained Mark 10:35 in this way:

> Jesus gave us a new norm of greatness. If you want to be important—wonderful. If you want to be recognized—wonderful. If you want to be great—wonderful. But recognize that he who is greatest among you shall be your servant. That's a new definition of greatness... That definition of greatness, it means that everybody can be great, because everybody can serve. You don't have to have a college degree to serve. You don't have to make your subject and your verb agree to serve. You don't have to know about Plato and Aristotle to serve. You don't have to know Einstein's theory of relativity to serve. You don't have to know the second theory of thermodynamics in physics to serve. You only need a heart full of grace, a

soul generated by love. And you can be that servant.[7]

I have come to understand greatness and success as
rooted in the pursuit of the good, the peaceful, and the holy.
Regardless of the goal of achievement, there is no greater
outcome in reaching that goal than to have a peace of mind
that is discovered when serving others in humility with
love. These values make our lives priceless, not only in
terms of self-fulfillment but for the common good. Albert
Einstein once said, "Try not to become a [wo]man of success
but rather try to become a [wo]man of value." These values
are enduring and legacy-bearing toward the common good.
More importantly, to do something for the right reason
means more than the fruit that it might produce. In fact,
when the root is healthy and strong, the fruit will also be
appropriately good. When we serve for the right reason—
that is, to help others—we will reap goodness along with
them. But, the focus of goodwill is not on us. It is on them!

Don't Get Your Butt on Your Shoulders

There are at least two ways to think of *focus*. As stated above,
there is the focus of goodwill, but also there is the focus of
ill will. We have goodwill when we aim to serve the other
for common good. But, I think of ill will as self-aggrandizement. Some people are all about themselves. They tend to
trample on others to get what they want. That is not the way
to achieve our destiny. When we are doing it God's way, we
are more concerned about others than ourselves.

Also, there is what I call religious arrogance. Some people serve others to prove that they are holy or right. That is

also the wrong idea. When we focus on others with intentions to accentuate our own value and righteousness, our service is as corrupt as the ones who don't do anything at all to help others. Of course, those who are on the receiving end benefit far more than the self-righteous giver. It is extremely important that we serve with humility with a focus of goodwill. We forfeit our own mercy from God when we fail to act humbly in service. True religion is not that of arrogant duty to others; it is that of kindness and gentleness of heart, truly embodying the old saying, "there, but for the grace of God, go I."

My earlier reference to Luke 18:9-14 seems appropriate here. The Pharisee in Jesus' parable thinks that, because of his educational accomplishments, religious position, and ecclesial accoutrements, he is fit for the Master's use. The great tragedy is when he views himself as better than other sinners, pointing out the other ordinary guy on the other side of the room, the rough-looking sinner. The Pharisee points out his own faithfulness and service to the Lord. In his self-appraisal, he distances himself specifically from the guy on the other side who is a tax collector. In urban vernacular, one would describe the religious man as having his butt on his shoulders. Morally and religiously, he thinks that he is what we may term as a "goody two-shoes."

It is important to explain that the tax collectors were not well-liked among the Jews. They represented the marginally religious, low class. They were not typically members of one of the notable religious sects of the day. They were rather ordinary fellow Jews who worked for "the man," which was Rome. The taxes were used to help to build roads, develop legal systems, fortify security, foster religious freedom, and to provide a host of other benefits for the emerging Roman

Empire. However, there was little regulation for the tax collectors' job. So, they developed a bad name among the Jews for using their positions to overtax their own people and to embezzle the overage. So, by virtue of the tax collector's position, they served as embellished arms of Roman economic oppression for Jews. As Jews themselves, they cared more about their own gain than that of their fellow Jews.

But, in the parable, Jesus praises the humility of the tax collector and refutes the arrogance of the religious Pharisee. The Pharisee was self-righteous. He was overly confident. He was disrespectful to other people. He thought of himself more highly than he should have thought. He was arrogant and prideful. He looked the part. He had the right theological training. He had won public opinion. But, his butt was on his shoulder. Jesus said that God resists this prideful approach to so-called faithfulness and service. In this parable, God favored the man who had the humility of goodwill. He gave grace to the lowly, genuine, and sincere tax collector of whom we would say, "there, but for the grace of God, go I."

Don't Forget to Say, "Thank you!"

Some people seem to think that the world owes them something. It is arrogant to have an entitlement attitude. The Lord puts people in our lives to help us. When they do, we should never forget to say, "Thank you." Showing humility in gratitude opens doors for more support.

I remember once when my brothers and I were at a concert, performing as our singing group, *A7*. There was a soloist who sang well, but when he left the stage, he approached us backstage saying, "Go on and tell me I did good! I know I did good!" It was so off-putting. Where was the humility? And who would want to work with somebody who asks for accolades. A humble approach would have been for him to allow us to offer the congratulations for a job well done. In such a case, he should have responded, "Thank you!" If this guy didn't change his arrogant attitude, his talents and gifts would not be enough to help him to succeed. The world does not owe us success. Humility will turn the knobs; our talents can only get us to the doors. Again, as my parents always taught us, "Humbleness is the way."

1. Richard Gula, *Just Ministry* (Mahwah, NJ: Paulist Press, 2010), 106.

2. Ibid., 107.

3 M. de Voltaire, *A Philosophical Dictionary,* Volume IV (2nd Edition), (London: John and H.L. Hunt 1824), 77–78.

4. Bruna Martinuzzi, "The Most Beautiful Word in the English

Language: Humility." No page numbers. Online Source. http://www.clarionenterprises.com/blog/?cat=19 (Accessed February 11, 2014)

5. Bruce Lee. BrainyQuote.com, Xplore Inc, 2014. http://www.brainyquote.com/quotes/quotes/b/brucelee379708.html (Accessed February 11, 2014).

6. Gula, 108.

7. Martin Luther King, Jr., (February 4th, 1968) "Drum Major Instinct." No page numbers. Online Source. http://mlk-kpp01.stanford.edu/index.php/encyclopedia/documentsentry/doc_the_drum_major_instinct/ (Accessed February 11, 2014).

5

A WAY WHEN THERE IS NO WAY

*Success is to be measured not so much by the position
that one has reached in life as by the obstacles which he
has overcome while trying to succeed.*

—Booker T. Washington

JETLAG! IT'S 2AM, and I am restless in Nigeria. This feeling is rather familiar. This is not my first time on African soil. I have been here twice before. I remember the first time I came to Africa. I went to the Democratic Republic of the Congo in 2007. Before going, it looked like everything was trying to hinder me from going on the trip.

First, we had trouble with the travel agent. It was our first time dealing with the Cincinnati-based travel agent. He wanted us to send non-refundable security deposits by a certain date. It seemed like pulling teeth to build the team to go on the mission, plus the second challenge of getting the security deposits for the five of us who were planning to go.

When we finally got the team and the money together, one of our team members was unable to finish raising the money for the mission. So, she lost her deposit. Our team was down to four people. The nurse had savings that she was able to draw from. The teenager was, also, able to secure funding from a trust that a relative left for her to pursue education. Her dad agreed that this mission trip was both spiritual and educational for her. Because of this, securing her funding was much easier than it was for the rest of us.

Four of us would go on the mission trip to the Democratic Republic of the Congo. My mom is a certified kindergarten teacher. She loves the children of the world. Khadene Campbell (Taffe) is a registered nurse. I would preach in the open-air conference at a stadium in Kananga. Vivian Lennon, a teenager from church, would assist mainly with working with the children. We were so excited that we could hardly wait!

Then, on the day of the trip, the agent informed us that the plane was going to be delayed. They gave us the new time for departure. Khadene, Vivian, my mom, and I arrived at New York's JFK on-time for the newly reported time of departure. We had lots of luggage that included medical supplies that Khadene was bringing along for people who were suffering with hypertension and diabetes. My mom was also bringing lots of educational gifts for the children. She was looking forward to working with the precious children and leaving these gifts behind.

But when we got to JFK and lugged all of the luggage in, the agent broke the news that our flight to Paris had already left at the originally planned time! Because we would now miss our connecting flight from Paris and then to Kinshasa, we would have to wait five days before the next flight. How discouraging! This was our first trip to Africa! The challenge of securing a team, raising the money, and the hassle of going from West Haven, CT to JFK! And now, this!

Thankfully, Theresa Christmas, who lived in West Haven, CT, was our chauffeur to the airport. She helped us lug the luggage into the airport. So, she would help us to get it all back in the car while we scuffled and struggled to figure out what to do next. Was this a sign from God that we should just cancel the trip? After all, this was not the first challenge that we encountered on this trip.

We pushed that thought back in our minds while we tried to figure out our next steps. I needed to ask Theresa if my mom and Khadene could spend a few days at her house. The teenager lived in North Haven. So, we just needed to contact her dad and let him know of the situation. It was Thursday. We needed to wait until Tuesday before returning to JFK to try it again.

This meant that we showed up at church[1] on Sunday morning. The word had not gotten around concerning our travel challenges. People were surprised to see us. When people found out, some of them understood and were encouraging. Others, lovingly asked, "Do you think that this is a sign from God that you shouldn't go?" I remember thinking deeply about it, but my conviction was that challenges don't always speak a divine Word to destiny. When something is God's will, troubles and challenges come to abort destiny.

Then, Tuesday came. We returned to JKF as we did only days before. This time, we would make the flight to Paris. The connecting flight would be a tight one. When we arrived in Paris, our connecting flight had already left 45 minutes before we arrived. My goodness! While we knew it would be tight, we were prayerful that we would make it. Destiny was delayed again!

We would remain in Paris for another two days before the next flight to Kinshasa! The airport paid for our stay at a local hotel in Paris. I spent two days before the Lord. My mom was praying, too. We phoned Pastor Muka Muyaya, who had already made it to the DRC from Cincinnati, OH to let him and Mama Mona Pauline know that we were stuck in Paris.

Parenthetically, being stuck in Paris was not too bad though we were delayed in our mission. We ate some great tasting baguettes and went for long walks through the beautiful little villages near the hotel where we were staying. It was a nice, short experience in Paris. We wanted to go to the Eiffel Tower, but it didn't work out as it was further away than we were willing to venture, given our travel woes so far. After all, our minds and hearts were set on the DRC.

We considered whether there was handwriting on the wall, telling us to return to the USA. Ultimately, we determined that these were mere challenges. It was up to us to overcome them or to allow them to determine our decision. God was with us, and we knew that, soon, we would see the glory of God in the DRC. We believed that many people would be blessed through our persistence to pursue this important mission through the challenges.

Soon, we would board Air France in Paris to finish our journey to Kinshasa. Flying over the deserts was not fun. The plane experienced lots of turbulence. But, we were confident by now that God would land us safely in the DRC. And God did!

Upon arrival, I kissed the dirt. My eyes had finally beheld the motherland for the first time. It was a historical but, also, a spiritual experience. I had a vision to share the gospel in the motherland and a mission to the DRC. Persistence was the key to seeing it through. What if we had allowed the roadblocks to hinder our plans for the DRC Mission?

In this chapter, I wish to explain the importance of persistence when it seems that there are no other options, and you are ready to give up and throw in the towel.

Move Your But Out of the Way

Often, we allow circumstances and situations to get in the way of progress. They become excuses for why we never achieve or reach our destiny. As in our situation of going to the DRC, we had many challenges that tempted us to just give up. The story could be one of the following: we wanted to go on the mission field in 2007, but we didn't have the money; we almost made it, but we missed our flight and just said, "forget it;" we made it all the way to Paris and were halfway there, but after the series of obstacles, we just assumed that the trip was not meant to be; so, we just turned around and came back to the USA.

In our lives, we often meander in the deserts of "buts." Far too many people legitimize complacency with buts. Pastor J. D. Walker, pastor of Mt. Pleasant Baptist Church in Woodbury, Georgia and New Hope Baptist Church in Manchester, Georgia, preached a sermon titled, "Move Your But Out of the Way." He took for a text Luke 9:57-61:

> As they were going along the road, someone said to him, "I will follow you wherever you go." And Jesus said to him, "Foxes have holes, and birds of the air have nests, but the Son of Man has nowhere to lay his head." To another he said, "Follow me." But he said, "Lord, let me first go

and bury my father." And Jesus said to him, "Leave the dead to bury their own dead. But as for you, go and proclaim the kingdom of God." Yet another said, "I will follow you, Lord, but let me first say farewell to those at my home."

Rev. Walker explained that, when following the Lord, all sorts of seemingly important reasons would present themselves to delay our progress or to hinder our desires altogether. Yet, Jesus calls for a certain type of persistence that defies human comfort and even human reasoning. Relating Rev. Walker's message to this discussion of success, roadblocks are lined along life's entire journey.

Success is not for the faint of heart. Success emerges through the toughest and, sometimes, most painful processes. Stated another way, it belongs to those who are hungry for it. Such hunger urges us forward when accommodations are not good. Every time you look around, there is something in the way, but don't allow the "buts" to become excuses to turn around. Distractions are pale in the face of this type of hunger to pursue destiny. This is a type of hunger that kicks the "buts" out of the way. Obstacles turn into stepping stones, and challenges turn into opportunities.

Many of our challenges are self-imagined, and others may come from other people. As in my journey to Yale, social location and small-town-mindedness seeded certain inferiorities in my subconscious. As a result, in a way, I assumed that "it was not just for me" even though I wished that it was for me. I could not imagine actually going to an Ivy League School. Besides, there were too many circumstances in the way. They probably cost too much; there may be an entrance exam that I wouldn't score high enough on; I probably couldn't get in; I am probably not smart enough; nobody in my family has ever gone to a school like that; not a lot of black folks go there; I don't know anyone in my family nor in my hometown who ever went there. All of the probabilities were not substantiated with any evidence.

It is easy to convince ourselves of negative ideals— whether they are true or not. Have you ever imagined yourself out of something good? Have you ever talked yourself out of the idea of achieving? Then again, there are mean people who would speak negativity into our lives and pour ice cold water on the great ideas that get us all fired up to serve and influence the world in a significant way. In those cases, many people allow someone else's words to be their roadblock. We tend to allow negative, destructive, and oppressive voices to dictate to us who we are, whose we are, and where we should go. However, there is an inner voice all along, speaking to us and nudging us in a certain direction that seems contrary to resources, a road map, and a clear way forward.

It's funny how discouragement has a way of crushing our spirits and choking our purpose by design. Discouragement can come in different ways. On the one hand, others can discourage us by saying negative things or by demeaning our ideas. On the other hand, we can discourage ourselves. Sometimes, we talk ourselves out of our destiny. Fear grips our hearts. So, we convince ourselves that this is not such a good idea or, perhaps, it's not for me.

If we allow them, situations and circumstances dissuade us from pursuing our ideas and passions. The operative phrase here is "if we allow them to." We only have one life to live; we can't afford to allow life's challenges to crush our passions. We have to push forward, despite the odds. Discouragement will come to everyone, even the ones we think are the most gifted among us. We have to dare to deny denial and resist resistance even if it's all in our own heads.

Persistence means that our life-plan must be based on our passions rather than on convenience. There is always a good reason why you can't do this or that. George Washington Carver once said, "Ninety-nine percent of failures come from people who have the habit of making excuses." It has been said many times, "Challenges are inevitable but defeat is optional." Moses Onodua notes that there are countless numbers of people who experience worse scenarios than our own; so, enough with the excuses.[2] Onodua then advises, "We need to wake up from our slumber and take the bull by the horn."[3] This is our time to overcome challenges and remove the "I Can't" Syndrome.

The "I Can't" Syndrome Must Die

As a young boy, I remember reading a book titled, *The Little Engine that Could*, by Watty Piper. Various larger engines were asked to pull the train. For various reasons, they refused. So, the request was sent to a small engine, which agrees to try. The engine succeeded in pulling the train over the mountain while repeating its motto: "I think I can."

Let's determine that, if it's the last thing we do, we will fulfill our God-ordained destinies! Earlier, I referenced the story of the "Healing of the Boy with the Unclean Spirit" in Mark 9. I focused on the challenges of unbelief. Note that Jesus asserts a universal truth that is relevant to the issue of faith: "And Jesus said to him, '*If you can*! All things are possible for one who believes" (Mark 9:23, emphasis mine).

Jesus was teaching the father in the text and us that troubles persist when we acquiesce to circumstances surrounding them. In other words, *we don't think* that things *can* be different. Think bigger than the problem. Believe beyond the circumstances.

The "I Can't" Syndrome must die. In his famous campaign speech, "Yes We Can," President Barack Obama said,

> It was whispered by slaves and abolitionists as they blazed a trail toward freedom through the darkest of nights. (Yes we can) ... It was the call of workers who organized; women who reached for the ballot; a President who chose the moon as our new frontier; and a King who took us to the mountaintop and pointed the way to the Promised Land.

We gain inspiration from those who were before us.

The subtitle here is this: "The 'I Can't' Syndrome Must Die." Notwithstanding, history has proven that "can't" has been defeated long before now. My deceased paternal great-aunt and godmother, Cora Lee Gray, was close to my siblings and me. She often baby-sat for our parents. Whenever we complained that because of this or that we could not do something, she would reprimand us for saying "I can't." In her words, "'Can't' died a long time ago."

As I look in the pages of history and reflect on her common response to our complaints, I must say that my aunt was right! Many patriarchs and matriarchs before us did not allow challenges to paralyze their passion. They would not accept "can't" as a legitimate excuse. Also, if we are to succeed, we must kill the deceiving syndrome, the mindset that tells us we can't.

When I was in the first grade, the Manchester Elementary School administration wanted to put me into a speech class, but my parents rejected that idea. Although I had a slight speech impediment, my parents committed to helping me with my speech development. Who would have thought that today I would be traveling the world as a speaker and preacher?

Also, going into the third grade, my reading was slow, and I could not seem to memorize basic mathematical facts. My parents told me, "Antipas, you are smart, and you can do it." With efforts to draw the smarts out of me, my dad plastered big orange poster boards around the walls of my bedroom. He wrote mathematical facts on each of the posters (i.e. 2+2=4, 5+3=8; 4+5=9, etc.). Mom and dad instructed me to read a few of them every night before falling asleep and each morning until I memorized them. They would quiz me regularly. As I learned them, dad would remove them from the wall one by one.

While I never developed mastery of mathematics throughout primary school or college, I became competent in the subject. In college, I took my final math course with Professor Mike Searcy. He had a reputation of being the hardest mathematics professor at LaGrange College in those days. But, I was determined to do well in his class. Knowing my weakness in the subject of mathematics, I scheduled time to meet with Professor Searcy every week for additional help. In the words of my parents from when I was a small child, I told myself, "I can do this." I am now proud that in my last mathematics course in college, I earned an A-! My parents' encouragement and pedagogy proved effective in helping me to learn my mathematical facts. Years later, it helped me to achieve that A- in my last college math course from the professor with the reputation of being the hardest professor.

With Christ, We Can Do It!

In Scripture, Paul exclaims, "I can do all things through Christ who strengthens me" (Philippians 4:13). When he wrote these words to the Christians in Philippi, Paul was incarcerated in Rome for preaching the gospel. Having been mistreated and hated because of his faith, Paul had reasons to complain. Instead, while he was in prison, he wrote one of the most encouraging books of the New Testament.

Many scholars have noted the irony of joy amidst Paul's imprisonment. Repeatedly, he says, "Rejoice, again I say rejoice." One wonders, how could Paul have so much joy when he is treated so horribly for trying to share good news about Christ's love and salvation? In Philippians 4:8 he explains,

> Finally, brothers, whatever is true, whatever is honorable, whatever is just, whatever is pure, whatever is lovely, whatever is commendable, if there is any excellence, if there is anything worthy of praise, think about these things.

In other words, when we think negative thoughts, we self-destruct. Praiseworthiness and success are byproducts of a positive outlook that is conditioned by constructive thinking. True excellence emerges on the other side of the drive to convert negative realities into positive outlooks. Christ gives us strength to climb any mountain and to cross any ocean as we maintain a positive perspective, even through the toughest of times.

This is a lesson that I have had to re-learn many times. Since I was in elementary school, I have had lots of ambition. However, I have struggled with a deep fear of failure. In the face of my own self-perceived limitations, I have had to repeat to myself, "I can do it." The fact is that we all have limitations. Some of them are real and others, at times, are imagined but may not be true. In any case, as we condition our thoughts toward God-ordained, Christ-inspired, and Holy Spirit-empowered success, we discover that there is truly no mountain too high, no river too wide, and no achievement too far-reaching.

African-American history teaches us that the "no mountain too high, no river too wide" saying is more than a cliché. One example beyond slavery is the 1955-1968 Civil Rights struggle. I will briefly recall a portion of the story. It was December 1, 1955 when Rosa Parks was arrested in Montgomery, Alabama for refusing to give her seat on the bus to a white passenger. She was tired from a long day's work. She resisted the demands from the bus driver and the law enforcement officers to move to the back of the bus. Parks was arrested, fingerprinted, jailed by police, and fined. On December 5th, she stood trial and was found guilty of breaking the segregation laws.

That year, Rev. Dr. Martin Luther King became the president of the Montgomery Improvement Association (MIA). The MIA was organized due to protests against the incident involving Rosa Parks. African Americans decided that enough was enough. With Christ on their side, they could achieve their long-awaited dream for racial equal rights. Their Christian faith had sustained them through the sickening and suffering of slavery. They came to the conclusion that Christ was able to bring revolution to this revulsion of ridiculous and rambunctious racism that had oppressed them for so long.

On December 5, 1955, Rev. Dr. Martin Luther King, Jr. addressed the first Montgomery Improvement Association (MIA) in a Mass Meeting. King said,

> I want it to be known throughout Montgomery and throughout this nation that we are Christian people. We believe in the Christian religion. We believe in the teachings of Jesus... The Almighty God himself is not only, not the God just standing out saying through Hosea, 'I love you, Israel.' He's also the God that stands up before the nations and said: 'Be still and know that I'm God.'[4] [sic]

That day, scores of African Americans decided to boycott the bus for 381 days. Their feet grew calluses, but their faith grew tenaciously. They gained self-inspiration through songs that they sang together as they walked, songs like "Ain't Gonna Let Nobody Turn Me 'Round," "We Shall Overcome Someday," and "We Shall Not Be Moved." Day by day, African Americans were more and more determined to resist resistance and bring an end to racial bigotry and systemic injustice. They believed that God was fully able to bring an end to the Jim Crow Era.

Today, as Americans, we enjoy the fruit of African Americans' deeply-rooted, Christ-centered determination from the days of old. We must also cling to that same faith in Christ and muster up the necessary willpower to make our dreams come true.

The Race is Not Given to the Swift

Success does not happen overnight. In fact, it may take a little while, but speed is not the most important outcome. As they say, the turtle that makes it to the goal is praised more than the rabbit that hopped quickly but gave out of energy and never reached the goal.

To express this principle, I will share my mom's journey in higher education. My mom has always loved learning and has dreamed of excelling in higher education. She started her college studies at Albany State College (University) in Albany, Georgia in the fall of 1973. She finally completed her bachelors of arts degree at LaGrange College 16 years later in the fall of 1989. After starting college at 18 years old, she and dad got married in 1974.

She then transferred her studies to Columbus State College (University) in Columbus, Georgia. But soon, she was pregnant with my oldest sister. So, she had to pause her studies in 1974 and started again after I was born in 1976. But, college was too much with the two babies. This was compounded by a third pregnancy with my brother, Norman Andronicus. Mom decided to wait for a while and focus on raising her three children rather than pursuing her studies at the time.

However, she was determined to finish college, so she resumed her studies in the spring of 1984 after three more children were born: Miriam, Alexander, and James Alonzo. However, she needed to pause her studies again at the end of the year in 1984. That was the year that my parents founded the Christian school at our church in Manchester, Georgia.

So, with six children, the start of the school, and the ministry of a church, mom was a bit overwhelmed though she did not keep her eyes away from her own educational interests. In 1986, mom got pregnant again with my youngest brother, David Arcelious. So, she resolved to get her associates of arts degree (a two-year degree) in general studies with an emphasis in education from LaGrange College. At least, she would have something for her years of vigorous study. However, mom was not satisfied with this because she wanted to complete her four-year bachelors of arts degree. So, two years after David Arcelious was born, mom resumed her studies in 1988.

It worked out for her because of the generous support from our church community. A member at the church, Linda Carter (Freeman), was working the night shift at Hanes in LaGrange, Georgia. In the morning, when she got off of work at 7am, she would come to our house in Manchester and babysit David. This would free some time up for mom to go back to college to work on her bachelor's of arts degree. She had only one more year left on this 16-year educational journey. In 1989, mom needed to get up early in the morning—around 5am or earlier—to pray, study, and assist the rest of us in preparing for the day before going off to do her student teaching (part of the degree program).

During the summer of that year, mom doubled up on her studies. By fall of 1989, alas, mom completed her bachelor's of arts in early childhood education.

Can you believe that after my youngest sister, Mia Esther, was born in 1991, mom returned to college and completed her master's in early childhood education? She now had eight children, three college degrees over the span of 22 years, and a strong marriage.

To add to this amazing story, after all eight of her children have finished college, mom is completing her doctorate degree in instructional leadership and early childhood education! She has a passion to serve children with the best education. She believes in the power of quality education to change the world. What a story of true perseverance! I call it an exemplary story of success as a result of "stick-to-itiveness!" Solomon offers the following wisdom:

> Again I saw that under the sun the race is not to the swift, nor the battle to the strong, nor bread to the wise, nor riches to the intelligent, nor favor to those with knowledge, but time and chance happen to them all. (Eccl. 9:11)

From his wisdom, tradition has deduced the proverb as follows: "The race is not given to the swift nor the battle to the strong but to the ones who endure until the end." Stick with it, and we will win!

Stick-to-itiveness

Many people fail at their goals because they can't seem to stick to them. The contemporary gospel song, "Can't Take it," by James Lorell Moss (J Moss), comes to mind. A partial quote from the lyrics at the beginning of the song states,

> I'm only human and the pressure
> Is getting to me

I just can't take it no more
My strength has walked out the door
And it left me and told me

I can't go no more
I just can't take it no more
I just want to lay down and die

Then, J Moss creatively responds to the human situation of weariness toward the end of the song. A partial quote from the ending refrain echoes the issue of weariness in pursuing success:

You've got to take a little more
Your strength has walked out the door
And it left you and told you
It can't go no more

You've got to take a little more
You might want to lay down and die
Just know God hears you, He's near you
He's your only hope

The message here is clear. We must keep at it even when life takes sudden and uncertain twists and turns. It has been said, "If God brings you to it, He will bring you through it."

The Greek term for "perseverance" is *hupomone*. *Hupomone* means to remain steadfast or to act with tenacity, and it also means to thrive under pressure. In fact, the Greek term translates as "to remain under misfortune and trials."[5] *Hupomone* speaks to the struggle of achievement, a struggle that encounters great hardship, problems, resistance, or some sort of severe adversity. To put it in idiomatic terms, *hupomone* means "to learn how to take a lickin' and keep on tickin'." It means to turn hardships into learning opportunities. It means to gain strength in weakness. It means to keep moving forward and upward when you have lots of reasons to want to give up.

At another level, *hupomone* means to trust God when others walk away. The painful fact is that, sometimes, the very people we trust with our secrets—the ones who we think are "ride-or-die" type friends, the ones who we would stick our necks out for—are some of the very ones who will disappear in our most vulnerable times. *Hupomone* helps us to understand that neglect is not abandonment. God is who we need when God is all we seem to have.

Theologian and preacher John MacArthur notes that Christian perseverance in the Greek sense of the word is not a passive acceptance of any of the pressures under which we find ourselves. It is victorious, triumphant survival as a result of unswerving faithfulness to the Lord, even in the middle of struggles.[6] Scripture teaches, "The testing of [our] faith produces perseverance" (James 1:3, NIV). Even when it seems that others are going out of their way to hinder our success, their efforts pale in the face of tenacious faith and audacious perseverance.

Some storms seem to never end, yet God is not only the God of the calm; He is also more powerful than the worst storm. Relating storms to life, the challenges that we experience are only temporary. If we depend on Jesus, He will help us to reach our goals. Moreover, success is birthed out of a bit more than insistent tenacity and loyalty to God. It is the product of continued submission to God throughout the entire journey. In other words, we must put forth effort to praise God through the storm.

My mom used to sing an ole Andraé Crouch song, "Through It All." I can hear the melody in the corridors of my mind as I am writing. The third verse and chorus speak of "stick-to-itiveness."

> I thank God for the mountains,
> and I thank Him for the valleys,
> I thank Him for the storms He brought me
>   through.
> For if I'd never had a problem,
> I wouldn't know God could solve them,
> I'd never know what faith in God could do.
>
> Through it all,
> through it all,
> I've learned to trust in Jesus,
> I've learned to trust in God.
>
> Through it all,
> through it all,
> I've learned to depend upon His Word.

When God is on our side, we need to listen to Him. We will get there if we relentlessly follow His leading.

Put Your Back Into It

The English term, "relentlessly," must be understood correctly. It does not mean simply to keep doing something. The term speaks of intensity of effort.

Once, I provided a reference for a young lady who applied for a job at a local church. She got the job. Later, her supervisor at the church complained to me that the young lady was always on time and did whatever she asked her to do, but she took no initiative to go the extra mile. In fact, she would do what she was told, but her mind seemed to be in another place. In other words, she was doing what she was "supposed to do," but she wasn't doing it relentlessly.

Relentlessness means to go the extra mile, to do the job with your heart rather than simply to go through the motions. Some people seem to misconstrue the necessity of resting in God and the equal need of working hard. One should not cancel out the other. God gives us seven days in a week: six to work and one to rest. While resting is holy and essential to faith and personal success, resting does not constitute a "qué sera, sera" (whatever will be, will be) attitude. If we want results, we must have a strong work ethic, and we must pray without ceasing.

As teenagers, my oldest brother and I were close to our granddad. For a few weeks, granddad needed to clear off some land that he owned so that my uncle could put a house on the land. Being old school, granddad thought that, with my brother's and my help, we could clear the few trees and remove the bulk of the debris from the land.

It was summertime. So, granddad would wake up early in the morning—as he always did before he retired from the Georgia Rehabilitation Center (GRC)—to pick up my brother Duke and me by 5am. He wanted to work at the property and gain progress before it got too hot in the day. To do this, he needed us to be up and ready to work hard. He did not need sleepy-headed boys out there, pretending to work, nor did he need alert boys lackadaisically going through the motions. Although we were teenagers at the time, granddad wanted us to take up the axe or the chain saw like a full-grown man. He had a goal to reach. So, grand-dad wanted us to put our backs into chopping down the trees.

Success is not just committing to going through the right motions. Success requires that we apply all of our weight, energy, muscle-strength, and effort necessary to do the job as best as we can. This type of relentless persistence defines what it means to "put your back into it." If you are going to go to college, study intensely. If you are going to be an athlete, practice with all of your might. If you are going to be a teacher, prepare the best you can. Whatever you do, don't just go through the motions. If anyone is going to succeed in a thing, one must give it their all. In other words, "Put your back into it!"

Many years ago, I was exposed to Martin Luther King, Jr.'s speech, "What is Your Life's Blueprint?" It has left an indelible impression in my life. It was October 26, 1967, just six months before he was killed in Memphis, TN when King spoke to a group of students at Barratt Junior High School in Philadelphia. I will share only a portion of the speech here:

> In your life's blueprint you must have as the basic principle the determination to achieve excellence in your various fields of endeavor. You're going

to be deciding as the days, as the years unfold what you will do in life—what your life's work will be. Set out to do it well…

And when you discover what you will be in your life, set out to do it as if God Almighty called you at this particular moment in history to do it. Don't just set out to do a good job. Set out to do such a good job that the living, the dead or the unborn couldn't do it any better.

If it falls your lot to be a street sweeper, sweep streets like Michelangelo painted pictures, sweep streets like Beethoven composed music, sweep streets like Leontyne Price sings before the Metropolitan Opera. Sweep streets like Shakespeare wrote poetry. Sweep streets so well that all the hosts of heaven and earth will have to pause and say: Here lived a great street sweeper who swept his job well. If you can't be a pine at the top of the hill, be a shrub in the valley. Be the best little shrub on the side of the hill.

Be a bush if you can't be a tree. If you can't be a highway, just be a trail. If you can't be a sun, be a star. For it isn't by size that you win or fail. Be the best of whatever you are.[7]

In Colossians 3:23-24, Paul treats the theological significance of a strong work ethic. He advises,

Whatever you do, work at it with all your heart, as working for the Lord, not for human masters,

since you know that you will receive an inheritance from the Lord as a reward. It is the Lord
Christ you are serving. (Col. 3:23–24, NIV)

When we depend on the Lord for the reward and not on
human beings, we rest in Him. Also, we will be diligent to
present our best work. In time, the Lord will help us to produce good success.

"Take the Lawd along with You, Everywhere You Go. Honey Chile, You Gon' need Him!"

Jesus says, "Go and behold, I am with you!" The world is the
landscape of our assignments. There are many opportunities. There will be many avenues to get there. We can follow
a pattern, or we can write the model. We simply need direction, divine leading.

Along with many opportunities, there will also be op-
positions. Many times, opposition can be incredibly
overwhelming. It can take the joy out of ministry. It can steal
our hope. It can destroy our self-esteem. It can drive us to
forsake the vocation into which we know that we are called.
But, it has been said many times, whenever you bump into
the devil, you know that you are not going in the same direction.

The Christian faith promises that our God supports us.
Contrary to many life-stories and family experiences, the
Spirit of Christ is on our side; God is not against us. Psalms
124:1-3 states,

If it had not been for the Lord who was on our
side– let Israel now say—if it had not been the

Lord who was on our side when people rose up against us, then they would have swallowed us up alive.

In Matthew 28:19a and 20b, Jesus is saying, "I am with you! Now, Go!" Faith will carry us where money can't carry us. Faith will produce in us what our own perceived competencies can't. The wait is over; go! The excuses are done; go! It's your time. Go!

On my journey of vocational discovery, I would visit my home church in rural Manchester, Georgia. A mother at the church, Mother Juanita Carter, would always tell me, "Antipas, take the Lawd (Lord) along with you, everywhere you go. Honey Chile (Child), you gon' (going to) need Him."

Faith is a journey. There are many ups and downs. So, in the words of Mother Juanita Carter, "Take the Lawd along with you, everywhere you go. Honey Chile, you gon' need Him!" You are going to need him when your hopes are high, and you end up disappointed because things did not work out the way you expected them. You are going to need Him when people walk away from you when you need them the most. You are going to need Him when you second-guess your own advice to others. We need Him for guidance in all things.

When I was serving as youth pastor in New Haven, Connecticut, a young lady came to the Lord from drugs. She got a job and was doing well. Her mom was a mother in the church. The mother was so excited to reunite with her daughter with Christ at the center. The mother offered to relieve her daughter of some of the stress of juggling work and caring for her two children during the summer. Grandma decided to take her daughter's children with her on vacation to Florida.

The family came to church one Sunday and asked for prayer for their trip. I laid hands on them and prayed for their safe journey. By the next Sunday, the pastoral staff received word that the 7-year-old boy on whom I laid hands only a week before had drowned in the hotel swimming pool while on vacation.

What could mend a mother's broken heart? What answers would bring sufficiency to the questions, "Why" and "Why me?" What does one do when you are no longer reading C.S. Lewis' *A Grief Observed* but are observing grief first-hand? As a pastor, what do you do when a mother who just came to the Lord with excitement now questions the God that you helped her to get to know? What do you do when of all of the theologians that you have studied and the classes you have taken and the degrees that you have earned can't help? What do you say when Greek and Hebrew can't help? Knowledge about God seems to disappear in the anguish of the moment. What do you do when it seems that your prayers did not work? You feel overwhelmed with sorrow, grief, confused thoughts, and anger. You try to pray, but you worry if your own imperfections are prohibiting your prayers from reaching God's ears.

Life looks so big that you can't help anybody to cope with it. The problems are so complex that you don't have an answer. Words don't work anymore. Like the slaves on the plantation, moaning and groaning has become the best option. Where do we go? Who do we turn to?

A 95-year-old lady, Mrs. Rita Kitts from LaGrange, Georgia, was a precious lady who earned her bachelors of arts degree along with me from LaGrange College. At that time, she was around 80 years old. She had the mind of a young lady and could get around just as well as a young person. Mrs. Kitts loved my family and kept in touch with my mom. She would also call me to encourage me along my vocational journey.

Mrs. Kitts died at 95 years old. She was never married and lived alone. About two weeks or so before Mrs. Kitts died, she called me and left a message of encouragement. It was not surprising that she called. She had done that many times before, but this message was striking. She simply said, "Antipas, this is Rita Kitts. I have a word from the Lord from Scripture to share with you." With a faint voice on the voicemail, Mrs. Kitts read what seemed to be the first part of this passage: "from the end of the earth I call to you when my heart is faint. Lead me to the rock that is higher than I" (Ps. 61:2).

Now, I understand that Mrs. Kitts was prophesying to me as she was transitioning from this life to the next. The depth of her prophecy was profound and relevant to my hunger after God for life's best. Life is hard, sometimes very hard. If we only look at life's struggles and if we only watch the evening news, the ambitious among us will lose sight of who and what we feel called to do and to become. Mrs. Kitts was an angel that day. She brought a message from the *Psalms*, the best message of encouragement. The Psalmist identifies with the overwhelming need for supernatural intervention when living seems to take the life right out of us. He gives us some guidance when we don't know what to do in our distresses. He says, "Lead me to the rock that is higher than I." Thank you, Mrs. Kitts! In another place, David says, "I lift up my eyes to the hills. From where does my help come? My help comes from the Lord, who made heaven and earth" (Ps. 121:1-2). As Mother Juanita Carter put it, "Take the Lawd along with you, everywhere you go. Honey Chile, you gon' need Him!"

Anglican Solitary, Maggie Ross, said that Jesus' usage of the word, "behold," in Matthew 28:20 is a recapitulation of God's "behold" in Genesis 1:29. In other words, this is God's first and final call to us, the heart of the contemplative call. When He said it the first time, He shows us our pre-mortal provision expressed in seed-bearing plants. When he said it the last time, He shows us ministry provision expressed in the seed of Abraham, who is Jesus Christ.

The rest of the passage (Matthew 28:20b) says, "I am with you, always, to the end of the age!" I can imagine Jesus' disciples thinking, "Now, if He is going to leave us, how will He also be with us?

Luke does not end his Synoptic Gospel with "Go" because he was not finished. He has another volume. Before he gets to the "Go," Luke needs us to stop by Pentecost. So, he ends his first volume with "stay" in Jerusalem. He knows that we need power to "Go!" So, before we "go," we need to experience Pentecost! In Acts, Luke sees Pentecost is where God comes among us to be with us until the end of the age.

Just after the turn of the 20th Century, Bishop William Seymour of the Azusa Street Revival calls it, "a real personal Pentecost, the endowment of power for service and work and for sealing unto the day of redemption."[8]

At the turn of the last century, Pope John Paul II said, "It is the consciousness of the Lord's presence among us; by it we ask ourselves today the same question put to Peter in Jerusalem immediately after his Pentecost speech, 'What must we do?'"[9]

Biblical scholar D.A. Carson suggests that "Jesus promises to bequeath his Spirit to us, and he kept his word."[10] It is the Spirit of Christ that he is promising to be with us until the end of the age. As Mother Juanita Carter said, "Take the Lawd along with you, everywhere you go. Honey Chile, you gon' need Him!"

Pray Through

In *Holy Spirit, Holy Living*, I explain the importance of prayer in spirituality.[11] However, it is important to note here that prayer is more than a spiritual enterprise. Prayer, also, has practical relevance. John Calvin once said, "However secure [our] hopes may stand, [we] in the meantime cease not to pray, since prayer unaccompanied by perseverance leads to no result."[12] Prayer and perseverance are not antithetical. Idle hope and wishful thinking only lead to reflections on what could have been. Incessant focus and prayer without ceasing[13] are an incredible force for progress. Then, when we get to where we are going, instead of reflecting with regrets of inaction, we will reflect with the words of the Psalmist, "This is the LORD's doing; it is marvelous in our eyes." (Ps. 118:23).

Prayer invites God's involvement in the process. In the best case, prayer helps us to avoid certain mishaps. In the most difficult circumstances, with God's involvement in the process through prayer, we are able to make it through the uncertainties of the journey. Also, prayer conditions us for the arduous twists and turns ahead. In this way, the focus of prayer is not on situations but on us, the ones praying.

I have experienced the power of prayer. I feel its absence when my prayer life is out of kilter: my thoughts become cloudy, my decisions become poor, and my efforts become weary. My experience is that prayer conditions us to weather life's storms: when a deal falls through, when the promotion does not happen, or when things just don't go as we expect them to go. It is easier to walk away, knowing that our hope and help are not entirely the result of our own efforts (as valuable as it is to work hard). We must invite the higher power intensely (through prayer) to lead us in making our dreams come true. So, with all of our persistence of action, we must remember that there is an even greater need for persistence in prayer.

---

1. I was working part-time as director of the youth ministry at Cornerstone Christian Center in Milford, CT.

2. Moses Onodua, *Success in Business: A Systematic Approach to Business Survival* (Edo State, Nigeria: Freedom Publications, 2013), 83-84.

3. Ibid., 83.

4. Martin Luther King, Jr., "Address to 1st Montgomery Improvement Association (MIA) Mass Meeting, at Holt Street Baptist Church." On *The Martin Luther King, Jr. Research and Education Institute's website.* No page numbers. Online Source: http://mlk-kpp01.stanford.edu/index.php/kingpapers/article/address_to_first_montgomery_improvement_association_mia_mass_meeting_at_hol/ (accessed April 9, 2014).

5. See Joseph Henry Thayer, *The New Thayer's Greek–English Lexicon of the New Testament* (Peabody, MA: Hendrickson, 1981), 664.

6. John MacArthur, *Preaching: How to Preach Biblically* (Nashville: Thomas Nelson, 2005), 72.

7. Martin Luther King, Jr. "What is Your Life's Blueprint?" No page numbers. Online source: http://seattletimes.com/special/mlk/king/words/blueprint.html (accessed February 27, 2014).

8. William J. Seymour. "The Apostolic Faith (1906-1908)" and "The Doctrines and Disciplines of the Azusa Street Apostolic Mission of Los Angeles, CA with Scripture Readings (1915)." In *A Reader in Pentecostal Theology: Voices from the First Generation.* Edited by Douglass Gordon Jacobsen (Indiana University Press, 2006), 48-49.

9. Pope John Paul II. "Apostolic Letter Novo Millennio Ineunte of His Holiness Pope John Paul II to the Bishops Clergy and Lay Faithful at the Close of the Great Jubilee of the Year 2000." No page numbers. Online Source: http://www.vatican.va/holy_father/john_paul_ii/apost_letters/documents/hf_jp-ii_apl_20010106_novo-millennio-ineunte_en.html (accessed May 2, 2014).

10. D. A. Carson, *Becoming Conversant with the Emerging Church: Understanding a Movement and Its Implications* (Grand Rapids: Zondervan, 2005), 218-221.

11. Antipas L. Harris, *Holy Spirit, Holy Living: Toward a Practical Theology of Holiness for Twenty-first Century Churches* (Eugene, OR: Wipf and Stock, 2013), 94-95.

12. John Calvin, *Institutes of the Christian Religion: Of Prayer–A Perpetual Exercise of Faith.* Translated by Henry Beveridge (1845). Chapter 52. No page numbers. Online Source: http://biblehub.com/library/calvin/of_prayer--a_perpetual_exercise_of_faith/chapter_52_but_if_our.htm (accessed April 30, 2014).

13. 1 Thessalonians 5:17.

6

CONNECTING WITH THE RIGHT PEOPLE

You have to do the research. If you don't know about something, then you ask the right people who do.

—Spike Lee

I AM THE SECOND CHILD, the oldest son among seven siblings. We lived with our parents in Manchester, Georgia, a rural town near the western part of the state. Being a small town, there were limited career opportunities. Many ambitious young people from small towns would migrate to the cities where there seemed to be greater chances to advance in life. However, there are those who can't make that move on their own.

Yet, there are things that even folks in rural and other types of disadvantaged situations could do. Those things would vary from situation to situation. Our family spent a lot of time bonding as a family, developing our spirituality, seeking out a quality education, and working hard. These are all key values to success. Yet, many people would put a check by each of these same good qualities and say, "But, there is something missing." Guess what. I agree!

The principles that are discussed in the previous chapters are absolutely integral to success. Altogether, they hinge, however, upon one other crucial element. Faith without it is dead. Vision without it is meaningless. Education without it is mute. Humility without it is invalid. Persistence without it is vain aggression.

This is a two-word feature that transforms all of these ideals into virtues. The two words are "right connections." We absolutely need the right connections to succeed. Without connections, faith has nothing to work with, vision has no provision, education has no access, humility has no superior, and persistence has no directive. The journey of embarrassing failure as well as the journey of insurmountable success depends heavily upon those with whom we are connected. This chapter explains the essential role that connecting with the right people has in getting us where we need to go.

You have probably heard it said before: "It's all in who you know." There is a lot of truth to that adage. Who we know is just as important (or, even more important) than what we know. Primarily, as Christians, we need to establish a relationship with God. Indeed, promotion comes from the Lord (ref. Psalms 75:5). Yet, God uses people to help us. This is His creative order. God created us to be in community with people. So, don't sing the song, "As long as I got King Jesus, I don't need nobody else," unless you are depending on Jesus to help you to connect with the right people. The fact is that we need other people.

I am grateful for parents who understood the need to make right connections. They sought out opportunities to expose my siblings and me beyond the confines of our limited exposure in Manchester, Georgia. For example, we loved Gospel music and played music for the church. We formed a group called the A Boys and Girls Gospel Singers. The group comprised of five of my siblings; my god-brother, Antonio; god-sister, Elaine Childs (Parks); and me. All six of the boys' names started with the letter "A": Antonio, Antipas, N. Andronicus, Alexander, J. Alonzo, and D. Arcelious. The sisters' names are Naomi, Miriam, and Elaine. The A Boys and Girls would sing from church to church, primarily in the tri-county areas of Meriwether, Talbot, and Troup Counties and in Columbus, Georgia where Grandma Ruby lives. We wanted to record a CD and to go on national television, but we knew that the connections to make that happen were less likely to be found in the rural circles where we lived and ministered. We needed the right connections for that.

So, when Dr. Bobby Jones and the "Bobby Jones Gospel Explosion" from BET came to Atlanta, Georgia, we went to the show. Manchester was only an hour and a half from Atlanta. We were so excited! We understood that when opportunity presents itself, we needed preparation to secure the connection. So, we took our VHS tape to the show with us. Our sole goal was to work this opportunity to connect with the right person to get our tape in Dr. Bobby Jones' hands. This would be our key connection to enter the Gospel Music Industry! We convinced the security to escort us to the right person that would help us to get our VHS tape directly into Dr. Jones' hands. Indeed, that ole saying was true for us: "When you make one step, He [God] will make two." We connected with Dr. Jones personally. The next year, we were on the "Bobby Jones Gospel Show!"

We built invaluable relationships throughout the industry that have lasted until this day. Dr. Jones remains a dear friend of our family and has even come to rural Georgia on several occasions to support our family. In 1997, the A Boys and Girls Gospel Singers became simply A Boys. Later, we changed the name to A7. Building upon those childhood connections in the music industry elevated us to a record contract. Our song, "Don't Walk Away," landed on the Billboard Charts for 22 weeks. Many people have testified to how the song blessed them. People even reported that, at the brink of suicide, "Don't Walk Away" saved their lives. Again, the right connections are crucial to success.

Admittedly, I have not always taken advantage of meaningful connections. When we are young, we often lack discernment as to whom we should connect with. Young people tend to want to be friends with or look up to people whom we probably shouldn't. For example, each time I go into my office at the university and see my photo with Archbishop Desmond Tutu, I remember that his son lived next door to me when I studied at Emory University. On occasion, the archbishop would come over. Because I was taking a course with him at Candler, I would chat with him briefly in the yard. At the time, my interests were on other things, mainly the young lady I was dating at the time. Now that I have had the chance to go to Johannesburg, South Africa, and spent time in Soweto, I have so many questions. I want to reach out to him in Cape Town and interview him for a project that I hope to write some day.

I only wish I had established my relationship with the archbishop when I had the chance at Emory, but I didn't know then what I know now. That was a connection that could have helped me later. Now, that may seem like a small thing. Perhaps, it is. Though, it does in some way show how we can let connections pass us by that we might wish later that we had handled differently.

The administrative dean at Regent University's School of Divinity was at my office. I explained to him my interactions with the archbishop in the late-1990s and expressed how I wished I had remained connected with him. Jeff Ludvik's response was, "You were young and didn't know." Jeff is right, but how great would it be if we would take full advantage of the opportunities to build meaningful relationships and sustain them over time. Some people grow old, never having sustained connections, and they die never having reached their potential. In pursuit of success, we must ask God for wisdom to connect with the right people to help us to get where we want to go.

The aforementioned are examples of ramifications of taking advantage of and not taking advantage of meaningful connections. Opportunities come and go. There will surely be multiple opportunities to connect with people to help us go in the direction of our callings. Certainly, a few failed opportunities to connect are less likely to ruin our destiny. God's grace affords us multiple chances.

The point of this chapter is to help us to discern "right connections" and to start taking advantage of the opportunities as they present themselves to connect with the "right people" for destiny's sake. In summary, there are two main types of "right connections." The first is connecting with others who are already doing what we want to do. The second is connecting with others who are heading in a comparable direction in which we are headed.

Everybody Needs Somebody

You have probably heard it before: "It takes teamwork to make the dream work." There is no successful person who got there alone. Human nature is not wired to succeed without other people. In "Meditation XVII: No Man Is an Island," John Donne explains,

> ...No man is an island, entire of itself; every man is a piece of the continent, a part of the main. If a clod be washed away by the sea, Europe is the less, as well as if promontory were, as well as if a manor of thy friend's or of thine own were. Any man's death diminishes me, because I am involved in mankind...[1]

In other words, human beings are interconnected. This is one main reason why family is so important. Family is not merely a means of entrance into the world. Rather, family is necessary for a human being's holistic formation. Later, I will share the extraordinary role that my parents have played in my life and journey toward success. For now, I want to mention how grateful I am for the role that my seven siblings, my god-brother, Antonio Owens, and so many others have played in my life, especially my church family from A House of The Living God, Church of Jesus Christ in Manchester, Georgia. I will never forget them. They have been my rock of support, sounding board for ideas, greatest cheerleaders, and gravity in times when pride wanted to get the best of me. I don't hesitate to mention them alongside any ounce of success that I enjoy.

Like on a sports team, when one person loses, the whole team loses. When one person scores the winning point, the whole team wins. It is important that the whole team works together. So, they pass the ball amongst themselves. Each person plays his or her own position. Each person brings something different but important to the team. The unified goal is to win. But, they have to support each other, cooperate with each other, and bring each of their gifts to the game in order to win.

Similar to the team metaphor, Martin Luther King, Jr. calls for the "Beloved Community."[2] It is a community of interconnectedness in worship, love, and support necessary for success. It is a community grounded in principles of Christian life and service to God and others. Reflecting on King's coined philosophy of the "Beloved Community" during the Civil Rights Movement, Charles Marsh and John Perkins point out,

> Removed from its home in the church, the work of building beloved community withered and died. Unanchored from its animating vision of beloved community, the Civil Rights movement lost its spiritual and moral focus. At the same time, it also became confused about organizing strategies. This is a little understood but important point.[3]

The relevant point on the issue of Christian success is that, in togetherness, there is spiritual and moral strength as well as noteworthy practical support for a vision.

By virtue of being created for interconnectedness, we yearn for community in every area of our lives. This includes the journey of spiritual, personal, and professional meaning. Every person who attains fulfillment in life has multiple people to thank for the constructive role that each of them played in helping them to succeed. It is true. Everybody needs somebody.

Community is so important. Lots of adages are appropriate here. From "birds of a feather flock together" to "association brings assimilation," the general idea is that we tend to be influenced by the people with whom we associate. The aforementioned proverbs can be applied in many contexts. I will mention a few of the important appropriations as pertaining to success.

First, within a childrearing framework, we need to be sure to monitor our children's friendships, particularly when they are young. At a young age, they are most impressionable as these are their most formative years. So, it is important that they have friends whose parents share our own values and philosophy for home training. Also, those children should share some common gifts and interpersonal connections. This will help to cultivate success in wholesome social, intellectual, and spiritual development. As with children, our road toward success requires that we attach ourselves with the right people, a team of people to help shape our journey. They must share our values and philosophy. If not, they can hinder us more than they help.

Second, within an economic framework, proper associations prove prudent. It has been said that your income becomes the average of your five closest friends' incomes. Our financial disciplines as well as creative ideas as pertaining to investments are inspired and informed by the company we keep. For example, when I was in graduate school, I started investing in a mutual fund and a Roth IRA because a friend introduced me to his financial planner who convinced me that I should begin investments and how. I had limited funds, but I had a financially savvy friend who had my best interest at heart. Upon listening to my friend and following through with the financial planner's recommendation, I positioned myself to succeed in building wealth over time. Having the right team means that we need people with us who have skills and expertise in areas where we are weak. They should be able to contribute something to us, and we should be able to contribute something to them. A reciprocal effect makes the journey exciting and mutually beneficial.

Third, associations are crucial to faith development. In my book, *Holy Spirit, Holy Living,* I point out the role of association in Christian formation: those who we associate with can influence our spiritual and moral development.[4] Jesus calls us to participate in His body, which has many interdependent members. As a body, we need to participate with others who are part of the same body as we seek to represent Christ in the community and in the world.[5]

Another metaphor for the relational nature of faith is the cross. The paradigmatic expression of the cross reveals that divine communion involves a compulsory inclusion of both vertical and horizontal relationships. The vertical represents our commitment to and relationship with God while the horizontal represents our commitment to and relationship with other people, primarily those who share in this communion of faith. The life of holiness is, moreover, necessarily formed in us through communion with God and others.[6]

Fourth, success requires an interdependent type of interconnectedness. One of my professors from seminary at Candler School of Theology and South African Archbishop Desmond Tutu insightfully explains, "We are bound up in a delicate network of interdependence because, as we say in African idiom, a person is a person through other persons."[7] Tutu discusses this within the context of inevitable communal destruction when one dehumanizes another. By the same token, there is inexorable success when one lifts up another. Whether spiritual or other forms, all success is birthed through interdependence.

The virtue of interdependence is not only an African ideal; it is a biblical principle. The Church is a community of interdependence. Describing the Church of Jesus Christ as a "body," Paul says,

> The eye can't say to the hand, "I have no need of you," nor again the head to the feet, "I have no need of you." On the contrary, the parts of the body that seem to be weaker are indispensable, and on those parts of the body that we think less honorable we bestow the greater honor, and our unpresentable parts are treated with greater modesty, which our more presentable parts don't require. But God has so composed the body, giving greater honor to the part that lacked it, that there may be no division in the body, but that the members may have the same care for one another. If one member suffers, all suffer together; if one member is honored, all rejoice together. (1 Cor. 12:21–26)

So, we need to connect with people who are interested in lifting us up. We discern who they are by looking for people who share our interests. Another way to say this is to connect with people who are going in the same direction that we are going. Wisdom compels us to spend our time with constructive relationships. Too many people waste time with people who mean them no good in relation to what they really want out of life. We can't afford to waste time with people just because we like them. The question is not whether we like them. The question is whether they are any good for us. Connecting with the right people and not just good people could be our ticket toward achievement. Because God designed us as interdependent people, connecting with the right people could help us to reach our goals.

This principle applies on a moral level of achievement as well as on a practical level of accomplishing tasks. On the issue of moral integrity, Richard Gula aptly notes, "Acquiring a Christian moral character is a cooperative adventure. Who we are as individuals is highly influenced by the quality of our relationships."[8] If we want to develop as persons, we should spend time with people who share that goal.

It is merely impossible to become, for example, tactful if we spend most of our time with rude-acting people. As creatures, we are, in part, products of our environment. In our heads, we *learn* what is *taught*, but in our living, we *become* what is *caught* (emphasis mine). The best way to develop tactfulness is through association with people who are also developing in this character trait. This principle is transferable into other areas as well. If you are in college, you should spend time with people who are studying rather than with people who are more interested in other things rather than studying. Their behavior will influence your desire to study, and their lack of common interest in school will influence your desire to study—or, vice versa. In short, we need to spend time with people who are going in the same direction that we are going in.

In other words, friends are essential to our career, religious, financial, and personal development. We must choose them wisely. Gula appropriately asserts,

> Friends influence our attitudes, values, and perceptions... Friendships are marked by mutual enjoyment and care for one another, a desire for what is best for one another, a commitment to seek one another's well-being, and the freedom that allows for growth at each one's own pace. The company of good friends enlarges our imaginations, and our friends teach us how to be with and care for others.[9]

By the same token, bad friends are unhealthy influences in our lives. Proverbs 22:24-25 states, "Make no friendship with a man given to anger, nor go with a wrathful man, lest you learn his ways and entangle yourself in a snare." Unhealthy friendships trip us up in our journey of success. They project their negative thoughts, behaviors, and outlooks. Friendships can either encourage or inhibit our ability to focus on God's best for our lives. So, choose friends wisely. We need genuine friends who will be honest with us with encouragement as well as with correction.

Connect for Climb

The issue of encouragement is a tricky one. Some connections are destructive. Like crabs in a barrel, destructive connections pull us back. They don't push us forward. There are many ways to discern constructive connections. They are people who go out of their way to help. They extend resources—not always financial resources, however. Finances are certainly important, but they will come in time. Some of the best connections are not "money connections." For example, other valuable resource connections could be invested to help us to develop our ideas such as time, wisdom imparted, and references to other connections that can help us move in the right direction. Some of my most valuable connections were these. I often think about life-lessons that I have learned over the years. Not all of them were words that I wanted to hear, but they were helpful. I will draw upon those lessons in the pages ahead.

Genuine encouragers are constructive encouragers. In other words, we don't just need someone who would approve everything with flattery. Solomon's wisdom teaches, "A man who flatters his neighbor spreads a net for his feet" (Prov. 29:5). We need prayerful and thoughtful people who are discerning, truthful, and encouraging. These people are positioned in our best interest, they pray for us, they are honest when they see trouble, and they maintain a positive outlook as pertaining to the direction in which we feel called. These people may not be perfect, yet they give thoughtful and wise advice to help us on our journey. They have gifts that we don't have. They have information that we don't have. We need their gifts, and we need their information. These people are friends, but their roles are more than friendship. They are mentors.

The mentors' role is not merely that of a well-wisher or confidant. They are in a position to offer beneficial help and guidance, so we need to position ourselves to listen to them. We do have uniqueness about us, and our journey is uniquely ours, but we don't have all of the wisdom and knowledge to get to where we want to go. Therefore, we must have mentors to help us along the way. In certain areas, they have been there and done that, or they have some useful information filled with wisdom to help us move forward.

African American poet Langston Hughes captures the essence of beneficial guidance in his 1922, "Mother to Son":

> Well, son, I'll tell you:
> Life for me ain't been no crystal stair.
> It's had tacks in it,
> And splinters,
> And boards torn up,
> And places with no carpet on the floor –
> Bare.
> But all the time
> I'se been a-climbin' on,
> And reachin' landin's,
> And turnin' corners,
> And sometimes goin' in the dark
> Where there ain't been no light.
> So boy, don't you turn back.
> Don't you set down on the steps
> 'Cause you finds it's kinder hard.

Don't you fall now –
For I'se still goin', honey,
I'se still climbin',
And life for me ain't been no crystal stair.

Hughes is brilliant to bring the nurturing mother's voice to bear in advising the next generation on the issue of success. The mother's voice seems to point her son toward a future that she might not be able to experience herself. But, like any loving mother, she draws on her own journey to give wise counsel to her son (in her own words and in her own way) concerning what it takes to succeed.

My Grandma Ruby would be an example of Hughes' mentor in my life. Grandma Ruby never went to college. So, her language may be broken. Her knowledge in my particular discipline is certainly limited. But, Grandma Ruby has enough "mother wit" from years of blood, sweat, and tears to give some nuggets of wisdom that would help me to navigate life toward where I want to go. We should listen to mentors like Grandma Ruby more than trying to explain ourselves.

Then, there are others who have a bit more life experience in the direction of our calling even if not in the specific area of our calling. They may not have read Plato's *Republic*, but they understand what we are trying to do or where we want to go. Importantly, they are committed to helping us get there.

Examples of mentors might include a relative, a college professor, a colleague, a pastor, or a community leader. The mentor is someone who sees something in us, wants us to succeed in attaining the goal of interest, and has the wit or influence to help us to propel in the direction in which destiny calls.

I have had several mentors in my life and career. Some of them were temporary, and some were long-term. Depending on what juncture my mentors have appeared—high school, college, career interests, etc.—they have been godsends. They motivated me through encouragement, but their support was more than kind words. Sometimes, their words did not seem so kind at the moment, but they were fruitful. Mentors say and do what is needful rather than what we want to hear. They are interested in outcomes more than output. They want to see that our intended goal produces the fruit of our intentions. They don't want us to face a dead-end, end up with nothing, or hurt ourselves despite our high hopes and hard work.

A Caveat: Not All Connections are God-Connections

During my early college days, my brother, Norman, and I befriended a young lady who was also a young teacher at Greenville High School where dad was teaching at the time. She was a recent college graduate, so we were in the same age group. She lived in LaGrange, Georgia where I went to college.

One day, she invited my brother and me to the apartment where she and her friend lived. We were young and carefree, to some degree. We loved to have fun and were excited to be hanging out with beautiful young ladies. We laughed, talked, and were acting silly. Then, one of the ladies had an idea to take pictures together. In those days, we used a Kodak camera rather than the digital ones we use today. But, like today, young people taking pictures was a sport for which we posed with added excitement. Needless to say, some of the sillier pictures communicated messages that were not really true. From the pictures, it looked like we were partying hard and really flirting, perhaps, inappropriately. However, reality was that those were just silly poses. Our time together was actually far more innocent than could be interpreted in the pictures.

The young teacher was all excited that we hung out and had a great time. She took the hardcopy of the picture to work to show to dad. As soon as he saw the picture, he took it from her and would not give it back. Of course, she didn't understand why dad did this.

Later, dad explained to my brother and me that, given our desire for success, we should be careful about who we hang out with as well as the kind of pictures we take. He was not teaching us to be "stuck-up" or to think that we were better than other people. Rather, he was teaching us to be discerning and to choose our connections based on our expected destiny.

Two important lessons emerge as I reflect on the above experience. The first is that, just because people share a single common value, like education, it does not mean that the person is meant to be a close friend. There is more to the issue of discernment than a single common interest. Let's consider Jesus' reasoning:

> For which of you, desiring to build a tower, does
> not first sit down and count the cost, whether he
> has enough to complete it? Otherwise, when he
> has laid a foundation and is not able to finish, all

who see it begin to mock him, saying, 'This man began to build and was not able to finish.' Or what king, going out to encounter another king in war, will not sit down first and deliberate whether he is able with ten thousand to meet him who comes against him with twenty thousand? (Luke 14:28–31)

Sometimes, we are blindsided by one or even two commonalities that others may have. In *Before You Do,* Bishop T. D. Jakes rightly points out that giving time and careful consideration are important to avoid making decisions that we will regret.[10] Jakes comments,

I can trace every success or failure in my life back to something I did or didn't decide effectively. Whether in the course of developing relationships, doing business, selecting investments, or accepting invitations, I've found a direct correlation between my location on life's highway and my decisions to turn, exit, stop or start.[11]

On the issue of developing relationships, for one reason or the other, we often go head first into relationships without the necessary critical evaluation, counting the costs, or even asking important questions. We tend to see the good and attractive faster than we see the other stuff, the deeper problems. Later, we discover that there was more investigation needed because there is far more to making good connections than what initially meets the eye. I will return to this issue of discernment.

The second lesson that emerges has to do with the issue of documentation. On the road to success, we should apply discretion to how we document ourselves. At first, this issue seems off topic to the issue of connections. However, within context, the picture that my brother and I took with the ladies was actually no harm. Yet, in the future, something that was innocent potentially could be used to form allegations that are not true. The question is, how do I want to present myself in light of where I am going? What choices should I make? What acquaintances should I make? What image do I want the world to see of me? Many people spend a long time trying to untangle their profile from images that they documented years before. This is particularly important in today's social media world. In one click, a documented image can be published for the world to see. What is that image, and what will it do for our future? While we cannot police every image, this lesson is something to think about and seriously consider as we build relationships and as we present our associations to the world. To be clear, the key here is neither fear of people nor arrogance as if we are better than other people. Rather, it's about discernment of associations.

We Need Discernment

Discernment is absolutely necessary at all times, particularly when it comes to connections. It is true that connections can get us what we cannot buy. It is true that people who "make it big" get there because of so many other people. It is true that all successful people stand on the shoulders of other people, but it is true that connecting with the wrong people could be our greatest pitfall. Connecting with the wrong people could be the worst decision we ever make.

As part of my theological training at Emory University's Candler School of Theology, I served as a chaplain intern at the all-women's Metro State Prison in Atlanta, Georgia. Each week, I offered pastoral care to women who were in prison but not always because they committed the crime. Many of them were there because they were with someone, often a boyfriend, who committed the crime. Because of the laws in Georgia as pertaining to accessory, accompanying person in a crime was often punished along with the person who was actually accused of committing the crime.

Among the inmates that I served were very young women. Some of them were facing up to 30 years in prison. Regardless of whether the inmates could prove their innocence, their association with a criminal landed them in a situation that perhaps they never thought they would be in.

Connecting with the wrong people would create big problems for our progress toward success. Usually, there are signs along the way that indicate when a relationship is unhealthy. Success depends on discerning those signifiers. Then, we must make wise choices to remove ourselves from those unhealthy relationships before they damage our paths to success.

The principle of connecting with the right people proves crucial for friendships, marriages, business partners, employees, social gatherings, study partners, and the list goes on. Proverbs 15:14a states, "The discerning heart seeks knowledge" (NIV). So, we must do our due diligence in every potential relationship.

We need discernment in every area of our lives. Frankly, no one can teach absolute discernment. Many times, as with most wisdom, it comes through experience, trial and error. But, we can only hope that we learn more from other people's mistakes than from our own. Observing others, listening to them as they tell their stories, and taking note of our own small mishaps can help to strengthen our own propensity for discernment.

Discernment is an inner-knowing that is sharpened through constant relationship with the Lord. That relationship with the Lord is two-fold. The first is through prayer and fasting. The other is the through the community of faith. Both the personal and the communal process of discernment are crucial in decision-making. I like to encourage people not to make a decision without praying and seeking the counsel of a discernment support team. The discernment support team needs to be a group of people with your best interest at heart. Even more importantly, they must be praying people, seeking the heart of God on their own behalf and on your behalf.

While God gives grace for new opportunities, life is short, and success is too precious to make too many unwise and poor connections. We absolutely need to make the right connections. Connections for success are like electrical connections in a house. If there is a bad connection, the electricity cannot flow through, and all of the electric appliances are negatively affected. But, when there is a good connection, electricity flows through, and everything that is connected to the electrical flow works properly. In a similar manner, wise connections have dynamic impact on success. They position us for opportunities to catapult us toward all that God has for us. I invite you to pray the following prayer with me:

*Lord, I need Your help. I can't do it on my own. Please
send Your kind of help in Your time. Send Your connections to position me for what You want me to do.*

1. John Donne, "Meditation XVII: No Man is An Island." No Page
numbers. Online Source:
http://isu.indstate.edu/ilnprof/ENG451/ISLAND/text.html
(accessed February 27, 2014).

2. "'The Beloved Community' is a term that was first coined in the
early days of the 20th Century by the philosopher-theologian Jo-
siah Royce, who founded the Fellowship of Reconciliation.
However, it was Dr. Martin Luther King, Jr., also a member of the
Fellowship of Reconciliation, who popularized the term and invested it with a deeper meaning, which has captured the
imagination of people of goodwill all over the world. For Dr. King,
The Beloved Community was not a lofty utopian goal to be confused with the rapturous image of the Peaceable Kingdom, in
which lions and lambs coexist in idyllic harmony. Rather, The Beloved Community was for him a realistic, achievable goal that
could be attained by a critical mass of people committed to and
trained in the philosophy and methods of nonviolence." The King
Center, "The King Philosophy." No page numbers. Online Source:
http://www.thekingcenter.org/king-philosophy#sub4 (accessed
March 1, 2014).

3. Charles Marsh and John Perkins, *Welcoming Justice: God's Movement
Toward Beloved Community* (Downers Grove, IL: InterVarsity, 2009),
25.

4. See Antipas L. Harris, *Holy Spirit, Holy Living: Toward a Practical Theology of Holiness for Twenty-First Century Churches* (Eugene, OR:
Wipf and Stock, 2013), 106–107.

5. 1 Corinthians 12.

6. Ibid.

7. Desmond Mpilo Tutu, *No Future Without Forgiveness* (New York: Doubleday, 1999), 35.

8. Gula, 78.

9. Ibid.

10. See, T. D. Jakes, *Before You Do: Making Great Decisions that You Won't Regret* (New York: Simon & Schuster, 2008), 13–30.

11. Ibid, 13.

7

HONESTY, THE BEST POLICY

No legacy is so rich as honesty.

—William Shakespeare

BENJAMIN FRANKLIN IS OFTEN QUOTED as having said, "Honesty is the best policy." We have used the language of "principle" throughout this book. Though, in essence, we mean the same as "policy" as Franklin used the term. Also, I use the term, "honesty," broadly as another word for "integrity." Integrity is an essential virtue that has the necessity of truth at its core. Without honesty, hard work will inescapably result in a dead-end. In this chapter, we will explore the foundational principle that is at the heart of honesty: living a life of integrity.

It has been said that, if we start well but don't end well, they will remember the latter more than the former. Our legacies are not about the way we start but about the way we end. If this is true, Shakespeare is spot-on when he says, "No legacy is so rich as honesty." There are many businesspeople and entrepreneurs who started with integrity but ended in scandal. This is also true as pertaining to any ambitious journey: from romantic relationships that begin with love and passion but crumble in infidelity, college students who begin doing their best in their classes but fail because of cheating, sincere and anointed pastors who launch their ministries with power and accountability but fall into financial embezzlements, and businesspeople who start businesses with integrity but fall into corruption. Dishonest gain renders failure at its deepest level.

Jesus teaches the importance of confronting the truth for its liberating impact. In John 8:32, Jesus says, "And you will know the truth, and the truth will set you free." Clearly, Jesus evokes that the relationship between truth and freedom is intricate. In fact, there is freedom in truth. There is bondage in dishonesty. True success is in freedom. Therefore, true success is rooted and grounded in truth. There are many people who work hard and gain a lot but are not actually successful. For instance, dishonest gain is not true success. If we are to be successful according to God's Word, we must pursue our visions with integrity.

Don't Fool Yourself

Before we can be true to others, we must be true to ourselves. Destiny is connected to that fundamental set of truths. Have you accepted who you are? We are not truly free to live out our full potential until we accept our true selves. The abundance of self-discovery emancipates us from self-deception.

Here are two ways to think of self-deception: 1) destruction of self-image and 2) convincing one's self that something is true when it is not. When I think of destruction of self-image, I think of the famous line from Shakespeare's *Hamlet* in Act 1, Scene 3, lines 79-83:

Polonius: This above all: to thine own self be true,
And it must follow, as the night the day,
Thou canst not then be false to any man.
Farewell. My blessing season this in thee.

Laertes: Most humbly do I take my leave, my lord.

Laertes was in a hurry to get on the next boat to Paris. Like many young people today, Laertes was weary of his father's insistent instruction. But, Polonius gave him one more last word of advice: "to thine own self be true." Some literary commentators suggest that Polonius wanted his son to understand the importance of living a life that is true to who he was born to become. To do so, Laertes needed to live a life that is consistent with his own innate gifts and intuitions. In other words, living loosely, partying, hooking up with dubious women, and wasting money would not only distort Laertes' own life's purpose but it would also be an embarrassment to his father. Although, licentious living tends to feel good temporarily, this shameless lifestyle would not be authentic to whom Laertes really was—not to mention that it leads to destruction in the long run. So, according to his father's assessment, living loosely would constitute self-deception or, simply stated, fooling himself.

Similarly, when we waste our time, talents, and treasures, we fool ourselves, which is self-deception. God has chosen us and has prepared us for a life of truth and honesty. As my parents have always taught my siblings and me, "Don't forget who you are."

Circumstances and misfortunes don't define Christians' value. Christ defines who we are as well as our success. Regardless of where we have come from, the important question of identity is this: Who are we in Christ? In 2 Corinthians 5:21, Paul says, "For our sake he made him to be sin who knew no sin, so that in him we might become the righteousness of God." Christ has imputed upon us new identity. If we are not careful, the former identity will impede our progress and obstruct our success. It is, therefore, prudent to maintain self-awareness. To rephrase the earlier phrase, "Don't forget who you are [in Christ]."

Often, young people suppress their own self-image to try to be and act like their peers. Sometimes, assimilation leads to detrimental ends. Trying to be like someone else is tiring and produces discontentment. It distorts our thoughts and disconnects us from our own sense of purpose. There is no misery like feelings and thoughts that are misplaced from one's own purpose! Divine destiny belongs to those who cling to their own purpose amidst many other people, things, options, and conversations. So, in Polonius' words to his son, Laertes, "This above all: to thine own self be true." Have you confronted yourself? Are you naming yourself? Or, are you allowing others to name you? What are you thinking about yourself? Are they positive thoughts?

South Indian advocate for the poor and one of the most inspirational leaders of the 20th Century, Mahatma Ghandi, once offered helpful insight on the connection between values, thoughts, and success:

> Keep your thoughts positive because your thoughts become your words. Keep your words positive because your words become your behavior. Keep your behavior positive because your behavior becomes your habits. Keep your habits positive because your habits become your values.

> Keep your values positive because your values become your destiny.[1]

Note that it all begins with how you think! Thoughts belong to the person who thinks them. Don't allow anyone to control the way you think! They may cause you to "fool yourself" about who you are and where you are going.

The second way of thinking about "fooling yourself" has to do with truth-telling. Motivational speaker and famous author Spencer Johnson explains, "Integrity is telling myself the truth. And honesty is telling the truth to other people." Perhaps, what Johnson means is that, many times, we live a lie. We tell ourselves things that we know in our heart of hearts are not true. But, as you know, we live in a society where we tend to say what we think others want to hear. For example, when we meet someone who greets us asking, "How are you?", we generally respond by saying, "I am fine!" We are conditioned to say, "I am fine," even at times when we know that we are not fine. We are not always honest with others, just as we are not always honest with ourselves.

At first glance, telling the truth is not something that necessarily seems to contribute to any kind of success. In fact, some of us think that to psych ourselves out would be best. That way, we don't have to face reality. In fact, some people do drugs for this same reason. They want an escape from the many painful truths of life. Drugs provide an artificial and temporary escape. We love what is fake because it may feel better and look more attractive. I have seen heavy set people try to wear slim people's clothes. I have seen people of one ethnicity convince themselves that they belong to another ethnicity. Somehow, they want to escape from who they are. Perhaps, it's because the overweight person wants to be slim but finds it difficult to lose weight. So, to think of themselves as slim makes them feel better about themselves. Perhaps, the persons who convinces themselves that they are not African American, Caucasian, Asian, Hispanic, Indian, or whatever cultural identity or ethnicity to which they actually belong see something about another ethnicity that they wish defined them. They know they can't change their birth identity, so they convince themselves that they are not who they are in order to make themselves feel more special as pertaining to what they admire in the other. This could be a language accent, hair texture or length, skin tone, etc. This issue is also present among people who seek sex changes. They are obviously not satisfied with their gender. The truth about who we are remains, regardless of how much we want to escape the facts of life through drugs or otherwise. To maximize our God-given potential, we must confront that truth.

Knowing the truth means to face the truth. At some point, some people will realize that they psyched themselves out to believe that attainment would give them inner peace and joy. We will discover that nothing truly tackles pain like the truth. No amount of money, educational achievements, awards, material gain, weight-loss programs, weight-gain programs, exercise regimens, men, women, jobs, or partying can do it. We can't heal from pain until we take the time to confront its root, accept it as a reality, and go through the process of healing. Then, the pursuit of achievement becomes more than a false sense of fulfillment. God's idea of success is liberating as it happens from the inside out.

Tell It Like It Is

We cannot live the truth while telling lies. Back home, there was a common adage, "Tell the truth and shame the devil." The idea was that the devil does not like the truth. So, to "tell it like it is" is in itself a godly thing to do. Even if the truth hurts in some way, there is sacred value in telling the truth. So, it's always better to tell the truth. Granted, at times, the truth not only hurts, but it might render negative immediate results. Yet, in the long run, truth is stronger than a lie.

Recently, a friend shared with me that, when he was in the military in the mid-80s, the officials called him in to ask him "a question." He gave an honest answer, but his answer relegated him to an "other than" honorable discharge. While he was discharged for telling the truth, at least he did not have to live a lie. Too many of us are living a lie as a result of saying what we think that people want to hear, rather than the truth. There is no long-term peace of mind in living out a lie. Each day, we must ask God to help us to tell the truth, even when telling the truth hurts.

My brother, Duke, has always been outspoken. His career, practicing multiple areas of law, including litigating, seems rather fitting. One day, at a house gathering, a woman invited him to taste a piece of her cake. She was so excited to share with him her baked goods. Being overly confident that he would like it, she watched him take a bite. Eagerly, he took a bite, but with great disappointment, he did not like it. The lady asked, "So, do you like it?" Duke responded, "No, it is not good at all. I am so sorry." While the lady was disappointed, she gained so much respect for Duke. She could trust that he would tell her the truth.

I try to practice telling the truth. It is a challenge because I don't like to hurt people's feelings. So, I work hard to follow my brother's forthright approach to life. I have come to learn that there is a way to posture ourselves to be honest and gentle at the same time. Truth hurts, but it also heals. We gain respect from others when we tell it like it is. Others may not like us when we tell the truth, but they will always say, "One thing about her [or him] is he [or she] will always tell you the truth." Truth-telling (with humility and love) is a valuable legacy to lead and to leave behind.

Importantly, honesty is not merely telling the truth. It means to earnestly seek to live a life fully formed by faith and commitment to the gospel of Christ. In other words, while there is something admirable about the person who tells the truth when confronted about allegations of immoral or unlawful behavior, at a deeper level, the noblest life is one that faithfully seeks Christ and is submitted to the rule of law (in so far that the rule of law is consistent with the gospel of Jesus Christ) and moral integrity. A picture of success is not the bold admittance to murder. That person might be honest in the confession, but that person's life is not necessarily formed by truth. So, telling the truth should be the by-product of a lifestyle that is developed by truth.

All's Well that Ends Well

Integrity, as with all other virtues, prevails and produces triumphant endings. If you have read William Shakespeare's 1623 comedy, *All's Well that Ends Well*, you would be familiar with the subtopic for this section. Like with most of Shakespearian comedy, *All's Well that Ends Well* begins with a light, humorous tone and wittiness. Then, there's deception and disguise, mistaken identity, family drama, and lots of mind-boggling twists and turns as pertaining to love and fidelity.

Helena, a poor orphan girl, pleased the king. He gave her the husband of her choice. She chose the Countess of Rousillonson's son, Count Bertram. Bertram was not interested in marrying this peasant girl. So, he left her shortly after marriage and fled Paris for Florence. He even gave Helena a far-reaching challenge. He told her that he would not love her unless she could get his family ring from his finger and become pregnant with his child. But, of course, this was impossible, given that he was far away from her. Bertram simply had no intention for this to come true. Helena was heartbroken because she loved Bertram so much.

Bertram tried to marry someone else in Florence that fit his desirable profile. But, Helena's love is clever. It drives her to Florence in search of her love. Disguising herself as the other woman in the middle of the night, Helena ends up in bed with her runaway husband, Bertram. Helena became pregnant. She also mysteriously exchanged her ring from the king for the one on Bertram's finger. Bertram did not even recognize that he just slept with his own wife, the one who he rejected. He thought she was with the other girl, Diana.

Soon, the rumor spread that Helena is dead. The king demanded audience with Bertram. Helena secretly followed Bertram back to Paris. In the meantime, caught in the error of his arrogance, Bertram told the king several lies about the situation of Helena, but the king noticed that the ring on Bertram's finger was the one he had given to Helena. Ding!

Bertram was caught. His arrogance caught up with him. Lying got him nowhere.

Prideful Bertram then realized that the virtues of love and loyalty are richer than arrogance and that integrity is more rewarding than lies. Cut to his heart, Bertram realized that Helena had met his challenge. Her clever tenacity touched Bertram deeply. He surrendered to virtue and vowed to love and cherish Helena forever as his wife.

Shakespeare's brilliant comedy teaches us that virtue prevails. Despite the twists and turns, Helena remained true to virtue and faithful in her pursuit. This story could have ended with sad memories of lost opportunity. However, it ends well, teaching us that the twists and turns of life do not have to predict negative conclusions. Commitment to virtue produces favorable outcomes. It's not how rough we start or how bumpy the process may be. "All's well that ends well."

When I travel a long turbulent flight, the most memorable moment is when the plane finally lands safely at the airport. Regardless of how urgently my heart may palpitate when the plane rumbles in rough air, the fear turns to joy at the moment of pleasant resolve. Conversely, God forbid that a long and smooth journey would have a heartbreaking, disappointing ending. In those cases, it is hard to remember the previous bliss of travel. Plainly stated, we quickly get amnesia as pertaining to the good ole days when things go awry in the end. Practically speaking, it is true: "All's well that ends well."

Regardless of how credible the hard work we do, vices can be the demise of success. There are well-known stories of men and women—from pastors to politicians, from entrepreneurs to athletes, from educators to engineers, and so many others whose lives rose to prominence—whose, due to the lack of strong value systems, worlds came crashing down. We must behave with integrity. It is right to do right even when no one is watching.

If, at first, it appears that truth and righteousness will lose, we must remember that these virtues are holy and, therefore, enduring. Virtues will always win, despite the adversity they encounter. As stated in the Introduction to this book, the integration of Christ-centered principles for success is necessary for holistic formation that produces sustainable success. Everybody has skills of one sort or another. Yet, not everyone possesses refined character that is endowed with Christ-like virtue. Corruption of character leaves a legacy of failure rather than nobility. Leaders who have done a lot of good but live by a frail value system leave sad memories of whom they had the potential to become.

However, leaders who have done a lot of good and live by Christ-like virtues flourish in that potential and leave a legacy of greatness. Dwight D. Eisenhower is often quoted as having said, "The supreme quality for leadership is unquestionably integrity. Without it, no real success is possible, no matter whether it is on a section gang, a football field, in an army, or in an office."[2] Lord, help us to live with integrity even when it seems so much easier not to and when our friends try to convince us to take the low road and just get by.

Don't Let Nobody Fool You

Growing up in Manchester, Georgia, we used to say to each other, "Don't let nobody fool you. You might get by, but you won't get away." This proverb suggests that, if we think that doing the wrong thing will afford some sort of advantage, we are terribly deceived. In other words, corruption may give a counterfeit sense of advancement, but time will reveal that, all along, we have been marking time with no true progress at all. It's kind of like the citizens who lie on their income taxes. At first, it appears that cheating the IRS achieves financial gain. Then, the day comes when the IRS sends the auditor. The penalty of corruption is far worse than the false sense of gain. Where there is deception, there is no true success.

Short-term advantages blind us to think that we can somehow skate by without being caught. In the long run, however, we will undoubtedly discover that it was better to act with integrity even when it seemed to short-circuit the pathway to success. When one finally discovers this after being dishonest for so long, it may be too late to correct the indiscretion. As a result, an indelible legacy of dishonesty will be left despite the years of hard work.

Recently, a pastor, Rev. Vargis Upadeshi of India, sent an email to several of his friends, offering wise counsel to pastors as he lamented the many pastors who have built ministries that ended in tremendous heartbreak. Rev. Upadeshi says,

> I write this with great pain. Tears flowing. With due respect, let me plead you – "Please be careful – with power, money, and woman – It can catch up someday. Take a day off and search our actions – secret, private – and accounts. Let not my name fly in the Internet tomorrow. Let each one of us walk cautiously and keep our accounts clean, update – no hide and seek. If the intelligence officers will be at your (and mine) door to

see our accounts carefully, will we be caught? Is there anything that should not have happened? Forward this to those whom you love – all you love and are in the leadership. (email sent February 22, 2014) [*Sic*]

Indeed, there is much more to discuss on the issue of success. Yet, a universal truth emerges from Rev. Upadeshi's letter: there is no authentic success without sound, ethical principles. A holistic, Christ-centered success begins and ends with faith, vision, education, humility, persistence, the right connections, and honesty. As I bring this discussion to a close, I offer the following words from Maya Angelou's "A Brave and Startling Truth":

> When we come to it
> We, this people, on this wayward, floating body
> Created on this earth, of this earth
> Have the power to fashion for this earth
> A climate where every man and every woman
> Can live freely without sanctimonious piety
> Without crippling fear
> When we come to it
> We must confess that we are the possible
> We are the miraculous, the true wonder of this
>   world
> That is when, and only when
> We come to it.

May the Lord extend the grace that we need as we cling faithfully to faith. Let us study hard and learn all that we can. With humility, let us serve God and others. Keep pressing forward and upward, despite the odds. As we make friends, let's connect with people who are going in the same direction that we are going and those who are already where we want to go. The best connections are divine connections. May the Lord grant to us wisdom to live lives of integrity. With this, our lives are positioned for the pursuit of unstoppable success, not only for now but also for later. May our legacy be an indelible impression upon the sands of time.

---

1. Unknown Original Source. See Gandhi Quote "Your Values Become Your Destiny". No page numbers. YouTube Video: http://youtu.be/cFayOIUHJ-U (Accessed, June 9, 2014).

2. "Dwight Eisenhower: Leadership Case Study." "Leadership With You." No page numbers. Online Source: http://www.leadership-with-you.com/dwight-eisenhower-leadership.html (accessed March 23, 2014).